ODESSA

Facetten einer Stadt im Wandel

Facets of a Changing City

Joachim Baumann
Uwe Moosburger

ODESSA

*Facetten einer Stadt
im Wandel*

Facets of a Changing City

Verlag Friedrich Pustet
Regensburg

Die Publikation dieses Buches wurde ermöglicht mit freundlicher Unterstützung
der Graphischen Kunstanstalt Fr. Ant. Niedermayr, Regensburg
– der Stadt Regensburg und der Stiftung Ostdeutsche Galerie.

The publication of this book was made possible through the kind support
of the firm of Fr. Ant. Niedermayr, Regensburg, the city of Regensburg
and the Foundation Ostdeutsche Galerie.

Bibliografische Information der Deutschen Bibliothek
Die Deutsche Bibliothek verzeichnet diese Publikation in der
Deutschen Nationalbibliografie; detaillierte bibliografische
Daten sind im Internet über http://dnb.ddb.de abrufbar.

ISBN: 3-7917-1848-7
© 2003 by Joachim Baumann und Uwe Moosburger
Vertrieb: Verlag Friedrich Pustet, Regensburg
Englische Übersetzung: Carola Thielecke
Buch- und Einbandgestaltung: Astrid Moosburger
Bildreproduktion: Fr. Ant. Niedermayr, Regensburg
Druck: Fr. Ant. Niedermayr, Regensburg
        www.niedermayr.net
Buchbinderische Verarbeitung: Friedrich Pustet, Regensburg
Printed in Germany 2003

Dieses Buch wurde gedruckt auf EURO ART® matt holzfrei, weiß,
einem mehrfach gestrichenen Bilderdruckpapier 170 g/m", ein Papier
der M-real alliance Deutschland GmbH.

Guter Rat:
Warum man in Odessa nie auf einen Gullydeckel treten sollte

Good advice:
Why one should never step on a man-hole cover

„Odessa ist eine abscheuliche Stadt. Das weiß jedermann. Anstatt: ‚Das ist ein großer Unterschied' sagt man dort: ‚Das sind zwei große Unterschiede' und auch sonst sagt man vieles anders. Ich glaube aber, man kann auch viel Gutes über diese bedeutende und bezaubernde Stadt des Russischen Reichs berichten. Wohlgemerkt, es ist eine Stadt, in der es sich leicht und hell leben lässt." … schrieb Isaak Babel (1894–1941) in einer seiner zahlreichen Erzählungen über die Schwarzmeerstadt Odessa.

Odessa – was kennt man eigentlich von dieser Stadt, die auch die ‚Perle am Schwarzen Meer' genannt wird?

Gelegen an seiner Nordwestküste, ist Odessa die wichtigste Hafenstadt der Ukraine. Mit einer Million Einwohner kann sie zweifelsohne als Metropole bezeichnet werden. Ihr Name klingt irgendwie vertraut: Odessa – Odessos – Odyssee. Er klingt nach Bewegung und Wandel. Und genau darin mag mancher eine Erklärung finden für die Besonderheit, die in dieser Stadt zu spüren ist.

"Odessa is a dreadful city. Everyone knows: Instead of 'that's a big difference' in Odessa they say 'that's two big differences' and that's not the only expression they use that no one else uses. On the other hand, I believe there's a lot of good things to report about this important and enchanting city in the Russian empire. It is certainly a city where life is bright and easy." … wrote Isaac Babel (1894–1941) in one of his many stories about the Black Sea city of Odessa.

Odessa – what is generally known about this city, which in Russian is sometimes called the 'pearl of the Black Sea'?

Odessa, on the northwest coast of the Black Sea, is the most important port in Ukraine. The city is definitely a metropolis, being home to a million inhabitants. Its name sounds somehow familiar: Odessa – Odessos – Odyssey. The immediate associations are movement and change. This perhaps explains the special atmosphere of the city.

8

Die Bewohner von Odessa nennen sich selbst ‚Odessiten' und im Verlauf der Jahre hat sich eine stadteigene Sprachform entwickelt. Obwohl in Odessa Menschen aus über hundert verschiedenen Nationalitäten leben und Odessa zur Ukraine gehört, ist die Sprache der Stadt russisch, mit den – wie gesagt – typischen Besonderheiten und Eigenarten.

Die Odessiten selbst sind ein lustiges Volk, immer zu Scherzen aufgelegt. In der Stadt ist ein gewisser Frohsinn zu spüren, insbesondere am 1. April wird viel gelacht, da feiert man ‚Humorina', vergleichbar mit dem Karneval in Rio, den Narrenumzügen am Rhein oder der Basler Fastnacht.

Woher kommt aber diese sprichwörtliche Besonderheit? Der Journalist, Publizist und Mitglied des ‚Weltclubs der Odessiten' Jevgeni Golubowski meint: „Das liegt wohl daran, dass Russland schon immer ein totalitärer Staat war, im Zarismus und im Kommunismus. Und da gab es nun auf einmal eine Stadt, die sich in dieses totalitäre Regime nicht einfügen wollte, und warum? Nun, die Luft ist hier eben anders, das Meer, die Schiffe, Matrosen, Prostituierte, das alles machte die Stadt zu etwas Besonderem. Wichtig ist auch diese Vielzahl verschiedener Nationalitäten, die sich im Laufe der Zeit vermischten. Und es kamen Künstler aus ganz Europa, Musiker, Komponisten und Maler. Sie lebten hier viele Jahre und wollten nicht mehr weg."

Zu Odessa gehören mindestens drei Dinge: Der Primorski Boulevard mit der berühmten ‚Potemkin'-Treppe und dem Blick auf den Hafen, die Hauptstraße Deribassowskaja, zu der man immer irgendwie zurückgelangt, egal, wohin man sich auch wendet, und die zahlreichen, architektonisch bestechenden Kulturstätten, allen voran das Operntheater.

The people of Odessa call themselves 'Odessites' and in the course of the years the city has developed a language of its own. Basically, the inhabitants of the city speak Russian, in spite of the fact that Odessa is home to people of more than one hundred different nationalities and in spite of the fact that Odessa is part of the Ukraine, but the Odessite version of Russian is full of idiosyncrasies.

The Odessites themselves are a fun-loving people, always in the mood for jokes. A certain cheerfulness pervades the city, there is a lot of laughter, particularly on April 1st. On this date 'Humorina-day' is celebrated, a street festival comparable with the Rio carnival and the carnival parades in the Rhineland or the 'Basler Fastnacht' in Switzerland.

Where does this peculiarity come from? Journalist, writer and member of the 'World Club of Odessites' Jevgeni Golubowski suggests, "The reason is probably that Russia has always been a totalitarian state, both under the tsars and during communism. And suddenly, here was this city which refused to adjust to the totalitarian system, and why? Well, the air is different, the sea, the sailors, the whores, all this made the town something special. The great number of different nationalities which have blended over time are important as well. Artists from all over Europe came to Odessa, too, musicians, composers and painters. They lived here for many years and didn't want to leave again."

Odessa ist eine sehr junge Stadt. Nur etwas über 200 Jahre alt, hat sie bereits drei Leben: Das zaristische, das sowjetische und das heutige. Seit Mitte der 90-er Jahre des vorigen Jahrhunderts beginnt die Stadt wieder aufzublühen. Das ist an restaurierten Gebäuden der Altstadt zu sehen, die vorwiegend im klassizistischen Stil errichtet wurden. Ein weiteres Indiz ist die Wiederbelebung des einst so traditionellen Tourismus und Erholungswesens. Schicke Restaurants, Nachtclubs und noble Geschäfte ziehen vorwiegend die eher Wohlhabenden an. Es kommen ,Neureiche' aus den Ländern der ehemaligen Sowjetunion, Geschäftsleute aus Westeuropa sowie Gauner und Spekulanten von überall her. Der wesentliche Umsatz in Odessa wird durch Handel und Dienstleistungen gemacht.

Die offiziellen Arbeitslosenzahlen liegen zu Beginn des neuen Jahrhunderts bei maximal fünf Prozent, die Dunkelziffer ist um ein Vielfaches höher. Obdachlosigkeit, Straßenkinder, Bettler – auch das gehört zu einer Metropole mit westeuropäischer Orientierung. Ganz krass im Gegensatz dazu gibt sich die auf Eleganz stehende Damenwelt, die stolz und offen ihre weiblichen Vorzüge zur Schau trägt.

In a description of Odessa at least three items need to be mentioned: the Primorsky Boulevard with the famous 'Potemkin' Stairway and its view of the port, Deribasovskaya Street, the main street to which one somehow always returns, and the many cultural venues with their spectacular architecture, above all the opera house.

Odessa is a very young city – it is little more than 200 years old and has already had three distinct lives: the first under tsarist rule, the second during Soviet times and a new one beginning with the fall of communism. Over the last ten years, Odessa has begun to regain some of its former glory. This is visible in the historic town centre where the townhouses, most of them built in the classicist style, are being restored. A further sign of new life is the revival of the tourist and holiday trade which has such a great tradition in Odessa. Smart restaurants, nightclubs and elegant shops attract mostly the wealthy. The 'nouveaux-riches' from the various states of the former Soviet Union, business people from Western Europe and crooks and speculators from all over come to the city. Most of Odessa's income is derived from trade and the services industry. The official rate of unemployment at the beginning of the new millennium is supposed to be around five percent, but the real number of jobless people is far greater. Since Odessa has started reinventing itself as a major western-style city, homeless people, street children and beggars have begun to appear around the town. In stark contrast, the ladies of Odessa are extremely elegant, showing off their beauty proudly.

Odessa is therefore a place of contrasting impressions and it is fascinating to experience these on the streets, in the leisure and amusement districts, around the port or in the backyards – by day and by night.

10

So eröffnet sich dem Besucher in Odessa ein Bild zahlreicher Kontraste und es ist spannend, diese auf den Straßen, an den Erholungs- und Vergnügungsorten, im Hafen oder den Hinterhöfen zu erforschen – bei Tag und bei Nacht.

Bereits Isaak Babel, berühmter Schriftsteller und selbst ein Kind dieser Stadt, schrieb in seinen Odessaer Erzählungen: *„Odessa, mag der Leser sagen, ist genau so eine Stadt wie alle anderen auch, Sie sind nur zu engagiert. Stimmt schon, dass ich engagiert bin, vielleicht bin ich's sogar gewollt, aber: Die Stadt hat ein gewisses Etwas. Dieses Etwas spürt man als Mensch und man kann sagen, das Leben dort sei traurig, eintönig – alles richtig –, aber dennoch ungewöhnlich, ungewöhnlich interessant."*

Die Idee zu dem vorliegenden Buch entstand während einer mehrtägigen Fahrt mit einem Hilfskonvoi auf der Strecke Regensburg – Odessa – Regensburg im Mai 2001.

Isaac Babel, the famous author, who was born and bred in the city, wrote in his 'Tales of Odessa', "The Reader may say: Odessa is a city like every other and you, dear author, are simply not impartial. It is true, I am not impartial, perhaps I simply don't want to be impartial, but there is something extraordinary about the town. A human being can sense that there is this special feeling and though it is possible to say that life there is sad, uniform – all this is true – life is nevertheless unusual, unusually interesting."

The idea of writing this book was conceived while accompanying an aid convoy travelling from Regensburg in Bavaria to Odessa and back in May 2001.

The two cities have been twinned since 1990 and several times each year aid is sent to the Black Sea from Regensburg, the cargo consisting mainly of clothing, food, medical equipment and presents for disadvantaged children. These items are desperately needed in Odessa and, in spite of certain difficulties encountered with the border guards, customs and officialdom in general, they do reach their proper destinations.

In spite of the existence of these regular contacts, comparatively little is known in Regensburg and elsewhere about the 'pearl of the Black Sea'. We therefore decided to shed some light on the life of this intriguing city by combining photography with written information in the form of a book.

In preparing this, we were fascinated by the constant confrontation with all kinds of contradictory impressions: the old and the new, the beautiful and the ugly, the poor and the rich.

Odessa is a city of contrast. Contrast is ever-present. This book is an invitation to come on a journey to Odessa. In writing the book, we have made a very personal selection of what we will present. And, in keeping with the humour typical of Odessa, we would like to begin by giving a very important piece of advice for newcomers to Odessa, "Never step on a man-hole cover! It is probably insecurely fixed and underneath are the catacombs."

Seit 1990 existiert eine Städtepartnerschaft und mehrmals im Jahr gibt es diese Transporte aus Regensburg ans Schwarze Meer – geladen sind Bekleidung, Nahrungsmittel, medizinische Geräte und Geschenke für hilfsbedürftige Kinder. Diese Dinge werden in Odessa dringend gebraucht und erreichen letztendlich ihren Bestimmungsort – trotz gewisser Schwierigkeiten mit Grenzsoldaten, Zoll und Behörden.

Obwohl diese regelmäßigen Kontakte existieren, ist nicht nur in Regensburg relativ wenig über die ‚Perle am Schwarzen Meer' bekannt. Es liegt also nahe, mit Wort und Bild etwas Licht in das Dunkel dieser beeindruckenden Stadt zu bringen.

Was bei der Vorbereitung zu diesem Bildband so sehr fasziniert hat, ist die ständige Konfrontation mit Widersprüchen unterschiedlichster Art: Alt und neu, schön und hässlich, arm und reich. Odessa ist eine Stadt der Kontraste. Ihnen begegnet man auf Schritt und Tritt.

Dieses Buch lädt zu einer subjektiv gefärbten Reise nach Odessa ein. Und mit dem für diese Stadt typischen Humor gilt der dringende Rat für Neuankömmlinge: *„Tritt nie auf einen Gullydeckel! Er ist höchstwahrscheinlich locker und darunter befinden sich die Katakomben."*

Stadtentwicklung:
Von der Türkenfestung zur Millionenmetropole

The city's development:
The Turkish fortress that became a major metropolis

14

Historischer Stadtplan von 1888
Historic map of the city from the year 1888

Es beginnt langsam zu dunkeln am Abend des 13. September 1789. Ruhig liegt die türkische Festung Hadshibej am nordwestlichen Ufer des Schwarzen Meeres. Die Tore sind längst geschlossen, türkische Kriegsschiffe liegen gut verankert in der unruhigen See. Die Festung hat in der Bucht eine hervorragende strategische Lage. Hohe Mauern mit runden Wachtürmen und Schießscharten bieten einen guten Schutz gegen feindliche Angriffe.

Schon lange gibt es von der russischen Seite Pläne, die Festung einzunehmen und die Türken weiter nach Süden zu drängen. Der Zweite Russisch-Türkische Krieg ist auf seinem Höhepunkt, die russischen Truppen der südlichen Region stehen unter dem Oberbefehl von Fürst Grigori Alexandrovitsch ‚Potemkin' (1739–1791). In dieser Nacht soll Hadshibej fallen.

Von drei Seiten nähern sich Schwarzmeerkosaken unter Führung von Vize-Admiral José de Ribas (1749–1800) den Festungsmauern. Um vier Uhr früh, es ist der 14. September, beginnen die koordinierten Angriffe der drei Einheiten. Die Gegenwehr ist nicht allzu stark. Die Kosaken überwinden überraschend vom Norden her die Mauern mit Leitern, dringen ins Innere, töten ihre Gegner und öffnen die Tore. Die Festung wird binnen weniger Stunden erobert und die türkischen Schiffe außer Gefecht gesetzt.

Die russische Seite hatte lediglich fünf gefallene Soldaten zu beklagen, 33 wurden verletzt. Auf türkischer Seite fielen die Verluste größer aus – 200 Soldaten und Offiziere wurden niedergestreckt, alle anderen festgenommen. Erbeutet wurden zwölf Kanonen, 22 Fässer Schießpulver und der Harem. Der Held dieser Tage, José de Ribas, spielte in den folgenden Jahren bei der Gründung und Entwicklung der Stadt und des Hafens eine wichtige Rolle.

Denkmal des Vize-Admirals José de Ribas, Eroberer der türkischen Festung Hadshibej im Jahre 1789
Statue of Vice-Admiral José de Ribas who conquered the Turkish fortress of Khadzhi-Bej in 1789

The sun begins to set slowly on the evening of 13th, 1789. The Turkish fortress of Khadzhi-Bej lies quietly by the northwestern shore of the Black Sea. The gates have long since been closed, Turkish warships lie well anchored in the choppy sea. The fortress' strategic position in the bay is excellent. High curtain walls with round towers and arrow slits offer staunch protection against enemy soldiers.

For a long time, there have been plans on the Russian side to conquer the fortress and force the Turks to withdraw further south. The second Russian-Turkish war has reached its climax, the Russian troops in the southern region are commanded by Prince Grigori Alexandrovitch Potemkin (1739–1791). This is the night they plan to take Khadzhi-Bej.

From three angles, Black Sea Cossacks under the command of Vice-Admiral José de Ribas (1749–1800) approach the fortress walls. At four o'clock on the morning of September 14th the coordinated attacks of the three units begin. The resistance is not very strong, Cossacks with long ladders surprise the defenders by climbing over the northern walls, penetrating into the fortress, killing their enemies and opening the gates. The fortress is conquered in a very brief space of time and the Turkish ships are disabled.

Dieser Ort mit seiner hervorragenden geografischen Lage an der Schwarzmeerbucht war für das Zarenreich nun das südliche Tor zur Welt. Über das Schwarze Meer und das Mittelmeer eröffnete sich der Seeweg in den Atlantischen Ozean. Außerdem münden die großen Flüsse Donau, Dnestr und Dnepr in das Schwarze Meer, so dass mit weiten Gebieten Russlands und vielen Regionen Europas nun eine Schifffahrtsverbindung bestand. Es war die Weitsicht der Zarin Katharinas II. (1729–1796), die mit Befehl vom 27. Mai 1794 an José de Ribas den unverzüglichen Baubeginn eines neuen Hafens und einer Siedlung in der Um-gebung der ehemaligen Türkenfestung veranlasste. Ihm zur Seite stellte die Herrscherin den Ingenieur Oberst Franz Devolan. Dieser sah noch einen weiteren Vorteil der Bucht darin, dass hier die Schiffe das ganze Jahr *„mit allen Winden"* fahren können. Und tatsächlich gibt es nur an wenigen Tagen im Jahr einen extrem starken Wellengang und nur selten so kalte Winter, dass die Bucht gefriert.

Devolans Pläne wurden angenommen und am 2. September 1794 erfolgte mit dem Einrammen der ersten Pfähle für den Bau des Hafens die historische Grundsteinlegung. Es ist der Geburtstag des heutigen Odessa.

Allein die Namensfindung für die Ansiedlung ist kurios und witzig! Ist doch Odessa ein so ganz untypisch russischer Name. Die Legende kennt zwei Versionen: Wissenschaftler des zaristischen Russland behaupteten, dass es schon vor mehr als 2000 Jahren in dieser Region einen reichen griechischen Handelsplatz namens Odess oder Odessos gab. In Verehrung für Katharina II. schlugen sie vor, das südliche Tor Russlands zur Welt in ‚femininer Schreibweise' mit dem Buchstaben ‚a' am Ende zu versehen. So wurde aus dem griechischen Odess Odessa. Allerdings irrten sich die russischen Wissenschaftler, denn das alte Odessos lag nach neuen archäologischen Erkenntnissen nahe dem heutigen bulgarischen Ort Varna.

At the end of the operation, the Russian side has only lost five of its men, thirty three have been wounded. On the Turkish side the losses are far greater: Two hundred soldiers and officers have been killed, all others taken prisoner. Twelve canons, twenty-two barrels of gunpowder and the harem have been taken by the Russians. The hero of the day, José de Ribas, is to play an important part during the following years in the foundation and development of the city and the port.

The city with its outstanding position on the Black Sea bay became the Russian empire's southern gateway to the world. By way of the Black Sea and the Mediterranean, the empire gained access to the Atlantic Ocean. Furthermore, the major rivers Danube, Dnepr and Dnestr flow into the Black Sea, so that shipping connections were established with large parts of Russia and many areas of Europe. Tsar Catherine II (1729–1796), a ruler blessed with a great amount of foresight, issued an order to José de Ribas on May 27th, 1794, commanding the immediate beginning of work on a new port and city in the vicinity of the old Turkish fortress. In this, he was given the support of the engineer Major Franz Devolan. Devolan considered a further advantage of the bay to be the fact that ships could sail from here all year round, independent of the direction of the winds. Indeed, there are only very few days every year when the sea gets too rough to allow ships to sail, and winters which are so cold that the bay freezes over are very rare.

Devolan's designs were approved and on September 2nd, 1794 building work started and the first wooden pillars were sunk into the floor of the bay for the construction of the harbour. This day is considered to be Odessa's birthday.

The naming of the new city, in contrast, is mysterious and amusing. Odessa is a completely un-Russian name. Legend has two explanations on offer: Scholars in tsarist Russia claimed that two thousand years earlier there was a rich Greek trading port in this area which was called Odess or Odessos. They suggested using this name with an added 'a' on the end. This 'feminine ending' was appended in honour of Catherine II.

Blick auf den Hafen vom Dach des Hotels ‚Odessa'
View of the port from the roof of the 'Odessa' hotel

‚Djuk' Armand Emmanuel de Richelieu, erster Gouverneur von Odessa
'Djuk' Armand de Richelieu, first governor of Odessa

18 Überliefert ist auch eine zweite Version der Namensfindung. Die zur Zarenzeit vornehme Sprache am Hofe war französisch. ‚Odessa' rückwärts gelesen klingt wie ‚Assez d'eau', übersetzt: ‚Genug Wasser'. Aber genau das war nicht der Fall. An diesem Ort gab es kein Trinkwasser, es musste vom weit entfernten Fluss Dnestr geholt werden. Für die Gründung einer neuen Stadt war das nicht gerade ideal. Als man das Katharina II. erklärte, da lachte sie und meinte nur: „Dann nennen wir die Stadt nicht ‚Genug Wasser – Assez d'eau', sondern anders herum: ‚Odessa'." Ob das nun wahr ist oder nicht, die Odessiten sind stolz auf ihren Namen.

Der erste Stadtplan, von Franz Devolan 1794 buchstäblich auf dem Reißbrett entwickelt, sah eine Ansiedlung von rechteckigen Straßenzügen vor. Der Hafen mit seiner Anlegestelle und den Unterkünften für Admiralität, Garnison und Quarantäne zog sich wie ein schmales Band entlang des Ufers. Etwas höher gelegen und im rechten Winkel dazu entstanden die Gebäudekomplexe. Natürlich erfuhr die Stadtplanung im Laufe der Zeit Veränderungen, doch das Grundprinzip ist im Wesentlichen bis heute erhalten geblieben: Alle Straßen der Altstadt führen irgendwie zum Meer und je niedriger die Hausnummer, desto älter sind die Gebäude und desto dichter ist man am Wasser – ein gute Orientierung nach einer nächtlichen Feier!

Es dauerte nur bis in die 20-er Jahre des 19. Jahrhunderts, als sich aus den ersten kleineren Gebäudekomplexen und Hafenanlagen eine Stadt zu formieren begann. Einer der einflussreichsten Männer dieser Zeit war der im Jahre 1805 von Zar Alexander I. zum Gouverneur berufene Herzog Armand Emmanuel de Richelieu (1766–1822), ein entfernter Verwandter des berühmten französischen Kardinals. Ein Denkmal für Armand de Richelieu – die Odessiten nennen es kurz ‚Djuk' (englisch duke: Herzog) – steht am oberen Beginn der berühmten ‚Potemkin'-Treppe und ist eines der am häufigsten fotografierten Objekte von Odessa. In jener Zeit wurden die Grundlagen für die wirtschaftliche und kulturelle Entwicklung von Odessa gelegt. Die

And so the Greek Odess became Odessa. The Russian scholars, however, made a mistake: According to new archaeological findings Odessos was situated close to the Bulgarian city of Varna.

The following anecdote suggests a second explanation of how Odessa came by its name: French was the fashionable language at the tsars' court in those days. 'Assez d'eau' – Odessa read back to front – is French for 'plenty of water'. This precisely was not the case, however. There was no drinking water around Odessa, it had to be brought from the river Dnestr, a fair way away. This was not ideal for the foundation of a new city. When this was explained to Catherine II, she laughed and said, "Then we shall not call the city 'plenty of water – assez d'eau', but the other way around 'Odessa'." Wether this is true or not, the Odessites are proud of their name.

From the very first design, which Franz Devolan literally mapped out on the drawing board in 1794, the city has consisted of an arrangement of square blocks. The port with its landing bridge and living accommodation for the admiralty, garrison and quarantine was arranged in a narrow strip along the shoreline. Slightly higher up and at right angles, blocks of buildings were erected. Of course, over time, the plan of the city has been modified, but the main planning principle remains in force to the present day: All the streets of the old town centre lead by some route or another down to the sea, and the lower the number, the older and the closer to the water the house is – a great help in getting home at night after a party!

zentrale Rolle dabei spielte natürlich der Hafen. Von hier verließen riesige Getreideexporte das Land, hier gingen Handelsschiffe aus aller Welt mit Gewürzen, Wein, Stoffen und Maschinen vor Anker.

Nach und nach kamen Kaufleute aus vielen Teilen Europas und in ihrem Gefolge suchten Menschen aus diesen Regionen einen neuen Anfang in Odessa. Und so lebten und leben in der Stadt außer Russen und Ukrainern auch Albaner, Aserbaidschaner, Bulgaren, Griechen, Grusinier, Italiener, Moldawier, Polen – insgesamt sind es über einhundert Nationalitäten mit unterschiedlichen Religionen. Nach einem Erlass von Zar Alexander I. kamen vor 200 Jahren auch Deutsche, Österreicher und Schweizer nach Odessa und in die umliegende Schwarzmeerregion. Insbesondere die Getreidelieferungen aus den ukrainischen Schwarzerdegebieten machten den Odessaer Hafen zum wichtigsten in Europa. Im Jahre 1819 erhielt er den Status eines Freihandelshafens, der durch Zollvergünstigungen den Handel um so intensiver aufblühen ließ. Dadurch stiegen die Investitionen für die Stadtentwicklung sehr stark an. Die Bedeutung Odessas als eine exponierte Stadt im Süden des russischen Imperiums steigerte sich zusätzlich durch administrative Maßnahmen: Odessa wurde zur Hauptstadt des Novorossisker Gebietes und Bessarabiens erklärt. Generalgouverneur wurde im Jahre 1823 Fürst Michail Sergejewitsch Woronzow (1782–1856).

It took no longer than the 1820's for a city to begin to develop from the first small blocks of buildings and the harbour. One of the most influential men of this period was Duke Armand Emmanuel Richelieu (1766–1822), a distant relative of the famous cardinal, who was made governor by Tsar Alexander I in 1805. His statue – the Odessites call it 'Djuk' (from the English word!) for short – stands at the top of the famous 'Potemkin' Stairway and is one of the most frequently photographed sights of Odessa.

During this period, the foundations for the economic and cultural development of Odessa were also laid. The port of course had a central part in this. From here, huge cargoes of corn were exported, merchant vessels from all over the world, carrying spices, wine, cloth and machines, tied up here.

In due course, merchants from many parts of Europe arrived in Odessa and in their wake people from these various regions came to start a new life in the city. It is for this reason that the town is inhabited not only by Ukrainians and Russians, but also by Albanians, Azerbaijanis, Bulgarians, Greeks, Georgians, Italians, Moldovans, Poles – a total of more than one hundred different nationalities with a variety of religions. Following an edict issued by Tsar Alexander I, many Germans, Austrians and Swiss people also settled in Odessa and the surrounding region by the Black Sea two hundred years ago.

Fürst Michail Sergejewitsch Woronzow, Generalgouverneur von 1823 bis 1846, gab entscheidende Impulse für die Stadtentwicklung.
Prince Michail Sergeevitch Voronzov, governor general from 1823 to 1846 who had a major influence on the city's development

Die ‚Potemkin'-Treppe, Wahrzeichen der Stadt und weltberühmt durch den Stummfilm-Klassiker „Panzerkreuzer Potemkin" von Sergej Eisenstein
The 'Potemkin' Stairway, symbol of the city and world famous due to Sergej Eisenstein's classic silent movie "The Battleship Potemkin"

Mit der ständigen Zuwanderung aus allen Teilen Europas nach Odessa wuchs die Einwohnerzahl rapide. Mitte des 19. Jahrhunderts betrug sie bereits an die 100.000, parallel dazu stieg der Bau von Gewerbe- und Wohnhäusern, sozialen Einrichtungen sowie öffentlichen Gebäuden und Kirchen. Namhafte Architekten und Ingenieure wie F. Frapolli, E. Förster, F. Boffo, G. Torichelli und T. de Tomon wurden nach Odessa berufen.

Doch auch die besten Bauleute können ohne Material wenig bewirken. Und hier gab es ein großes Problem. Nicht nur, dass die Region um Odessa geringe Trinkwasserreservoirs besaß, an dem zur damaligen Zeit bevorzugten Baumaterial Holz fehlte es fast vollständig. Das Gebiet um Odessa war zu Beginn des 19. Jahrhunderts eine Steppenlandschaft. Und auch heute braucht man nur ein bis zwei Autostunden, um in Gebiete mit äußerst karger Vegetation zu gelangen.

Particularly the deliveries of corn from the fertile areas of the Ukraine with their rich black soil soon made Odessa the number one port in Europe. In 1819 it was granted the status of free port and the lower customs fees this brought about made the port even more successful. The investment in the development of the city therefore grew quickly. The importance of Odessa as a city in an exposed position on the southern border of the Russian empire was further increased due to administrative decisions: Odessa was made capital of the southern territory, the territory of Novorossisk and of Bessarabia. In 1823, Prince Michail Sergejevitch Voronzov (1782–1856) was installed as governor general.

As a consequence of the migration from all parts of Europe to Odessa, the population increased rapidly. In the mid-nineteenth century there were already approximately 100,000 inhabitants and, in keeping with the growth in population, the number of living and trading premises, welfare institutions and cultural and religious buildings also increased. Famous architects such as F. Frapolli, E. Förster, F. Boffo, G. Torichelli and T. de Tomon were brought to Odessa.

But even the best craftsmen can do little without building materials. And in this respect, Odessa was at a disadvantage. Not only was there a great shortage of drinking water, but the most popular building material of the time, wood, was nearly completely absent from the surroundings. The landscape around Odessa at the beginning of the nineteenth century was a steppe. To the present day, within a drive of an hour or so by car, it is possible to reach areas with very meagre vegetation indeed.

What was to be done? The solution to the problem also provided the city with one of its typical, unusual features. The area lies on top of a mighty layer of sedimentary limestone. This stone was quarried in blocks underneath the ground, then brought up and 'put together again' to form houses. And so, as they say in Odessa, the town was built out of itself. What has remained is a huge number of underground passages, a total of more than two thousand kilometres in length, which form a gigantic maze – the catacombs.

Was war also zu tun? Man behalf sich auf eine Art und Weise, die der Stadt ein ganz eigenes Charakteristikum verleiht: Sie befindet sich auf einer mächtigen Schicht aus Muschelkalkstein. Dieser wurde in Blöcken unterirdisch abgebaut und zu Häusern wieder ‚zusammengesetzt'. So entstand, wie man in Odessa sagt, die Stadt aus sich selbst heraus. Bis heute ist eine Vielzahl unterirdischer Gänge übrig geblieben, die mit einer Gesamtlänge von über 2000 Kilometern ein gigantisches Labyrinth bilden – die Katakomben.

In die Zeit um 1840 fällt die Anlage einer der schönsten Straßen von Odessa – des Primorski Boulevards. Er ist der Eingang zur Stadt vom Meer aus. Am Ende des Boulevards steht das im klassizistischen Stil von Boffo gebaute Schloss des Fürsten Woronzow, am Beginn die ehemalige Kaufmannsbörse, der heutige Sitz des Stadtrates. Die Mitte dieser von Akazien, Kastanien und Platanen gesäumten Allee bilden zwei viertelkreisförmige Gebäude sowie der obere Teil der ‚Potemkin'-Treppe mit dem ‚Djuk' .

Die Entwicklung Odessas in der zweiten Hälfte des 19. Jahrhunderts war durch die fortschreitende Industrialisierung geprägt. Der Anschluss an die Eisenbahn (1862–1865) war entscheidend. Nun konnten die Handelswaren von oder nach Odessa schneller und in größeren Mengen befördert werden. Innerhalb der Stadt begann man 1875 mit der Schaffung eines Straßenbahnsystems für Pferdewagen, die Anfang des 20. Jahrhunderts von elektrischen Straßenbahnen abgelöst wurden. Im Jahre 1903 erhielt Odessa nach Moskau als zweite Stadt im Zarenreich einen Rettungsdienst, die ‚Schnelle Medizinische Hilfe'. Zu dieser Zeit gab es in der Stadt bereits über 400 Betriebe und Firmen, dazu kamen zahlreiche Dienstleistungsunternehmen. Zu Beginn des 20. Jahr-hunderts galt Odessa als beliebter Erholungs-, Bade- und Kurort.

Bereits in der zweiten Hälfte des 19. Jahrhunderts entstanden viele kulturelle und Bildungseinrichtungen. So wurde beispielsweise aus dem ehemaligen ‚Richelieu'-Lyzeum, das 1817 gegründet wurde, die Noworossisker Universität (1865), die heutige Staatliche ‚Metschnikow'-Universität.

Around 1840 one of the most beautiful streets of Odessa was created – Primorsky Boulevard. This boulevard is the gateway to the city from the sea. One end of the boulevard is marked by the palace of Prince Voronzov, designed in the classicist style by Boffo, at the other end stands the former stock market which now houses the city council.

Half way along this avenue, which is lined by acacias, chestnut trees and plane trees is a half-crescent of buildings which forms the back-drop for the top of the 'Potemkin' Stairway with the 'Djuk'.

The development of Odessa during the second half of the nineteenth century was dominated by the advance of industrialisation. The construction of the railway line (1862–1865) was decisive. Now merchandise could be transported to and from Odessa more quickly and in greater quantities. Inside the city, 1875 saw the beginning of work on a new tram system using horse-drawn trams, which were abolished at the beginning of the twentieth century in favour of trams powered by electricity. In 1903, Odessa was given an ambulance service, only the second city in the Russian empire after Moscow to have one. At this point there were already more than four hundred enterprises producing goods in the city, with a multitude of others offering services. In the early years of the twentieth century Odessa was a popular holiday and health resort.

During the second half of the nineteenth century many cultural and educational institutions were established. The former 'Richelieu' Lyceum, founded in 1817, for example, was turned into Novorossisk University (1865), which still exists and is now called 'Mechnikov' State University.

Between 1884 and 1887 one of the most beautiful theatres in the world, the Odessa opera house, was built according to designs drawn up by the Austrian architects Helmer and Fellner. This attracted artists from all over Europe to the city.

**Blau und gelb sind
die Nationalfarben der
Ukrainischen Republik.**
*Blue and yellow are
the national colours of the
Ukrainian Republic.*

Von 1884 bis 1887 erbaute man nach den Plänen der österreichischen Architekten Helmer und Fellner eines der schönsten Theater der Welt, das Odessaer Opernhaus. Künstler aus ganz Europa zieht es noch heute in die Stadt.

Großbetriebe und der Ausbau des Hafens veränderten die Stadt. Eine völlig neue Periode begann im Jahre 1920, als die Sowjetmacht die führende Rolle auch in Odessa übernahm. Viele Ausländer und Odessiten unterschiedlichster Nationalität flüchteten aus der Stadt unter zum Teil dramatischen Bedingungen. Sie mussten ihr ganzes Hab und Gut zurücklassen.

Der politische Wandel und die geschichtlichen Ereignisse von 1939 bis 1945 sowie die danach wechselnden kommunistischen Machthaber trugen nicht zum Aufblühen der Stadt in dem Sinne bei, wie es im Jahrhundert zuvor der Fall war. Dennoch: Die Stadt wuchs mit den Jahren, Industrieanlagen und neue Wohngebiete in Plattenbauweise entstanden an der Peripherie. Odessa wurde zur Millionenstadt und zu einem der wichtigsten Wirtschaftsstandorte der Ukraine.

Wie sieht das Heute in Odessa aus? Welche Menschen trifft man? Woher kommt der Odessaer Humor? Welchen Kontrasten begegnet man? Kann man das „besondere Etwas", wie es der Schriftsteller Isaak Babel ausdrückte, in Bildern festhalten? Einen Versuch jedenfalls ist es wert.

Eine der spannendsten Straßen, die bisher jedoch noch keine Erwähnung fand, ist die Deribassowskaja. Sie wurde im Laufe der politischen Umbrüche immer wieder umbenannt, doch in den Köpfen der Odessiten war und ist sie für immer die Deribassowskaja.

The founding of major factories and the extension of the port changed the character of the city. A completely new period began in 1920, when the Soviets took power in Odessa. Many foreigners and Odessites of various ethnic backgrounds had to flee the city, in sometimes dramatic circumstances, leaving all their possessions behind.

Political change and the historical events between 1939 and 1945 as well as a series of communist rulers meant that the city did not continue to thrive as it had in the nineteenth century. It did, however, continue to grow, with industrial plants and new residential areas consisting of prefab high-rise buildings shooting up around the edges of the city. Odessa's population surpassed one million and the city became one of the most important economic centres in the Ukraine.

What then is present day Odessa like? What distinguishes Odessites from the rest of the world? Where does their sense of humour spring from? Which contrasting impressions is one faced with? Is it possible to capture the "certain something", as the writer Isaac Babel put it, in pictures? We certainly think it is worth trying.

One of the most fascinating streets in Odessa which has, however, not been mentioned so far, is Deribasovskaya Street. In the course of political change it has been renamed several times, but to the Odessites, it has always remained Deribasovskaya.

Deribassowskaja:
Man kommt immer wieder zu ihr zurück

Deribasovskaya:
The street you always return to

Die Deribassowskaja ist die Flaniermeile der Stadt. Restaurants laden zum Verweilen ein, bunte Schaufenster locken zahlungskräftige Besucher. Händler, Musikanten und Schausteller verdienen sich hier ihren Unterhalt.
Deribasovskaya Street is the place where Odessites like to walk out. There are restaurants to relax in and colourful window displays which attract wealthy visitors. Street traders, musicians and entertainers earn a living here.

Viele Straßen in Odessa tragen heute wieder dieselben Namen wie zur Zarenzeit. Als Folge kommunistischer Politik gab es natürlich auch in Odessa Umbenennungen und es ist kurios, dass heute, zehn Jahre nach den gesellschaftlichen Veränderungen, die meisten Straßen bei den Odessiten noch – oder wieder – zwei Namen besitzen. Für den Besucher, der die Schwarzmeerstadt aus einer Zeit vor zwanzig oder mehr Jahren kennt, fällt die anfängliche Orientierung schwer. Ist die Ekatarinenstraße nun die ehemalige Karl-Marx-Straße oder die Leninstraße? Wie hieß denn damals die Langeronstraße? Doch das gibt sich, denn die bereits erwähnte Gitterstruktur der einzelnen Straßenzüge und die Nummerierung der Häuser – absteigend in Richtung Meer und immer auf der einen Seite die geraden, auf der anderen die ungeraden Hausnummern – erleichtern die Orientierung. Bei allem anfänglichen Namenswirrwarr – bei einer Straße gibt es keine Probleme: Der Deribassowskaja.

Sie ist nicht unbedingt die schönste Straße der Stadt, an ihren Rändern wurzeln keine für die Stadt typischen Platanen oder weißen Akazien und auch mit den ältesten Prachtbauten, Theatergebäuden und schicken Hotels kann sie nicht dienen.

Many streets in Odessa have now been given back their names from the days of the Russian empire. As a consequence of communist policy, streets in Odessa were of course renamed and it is a curious fact that at present, ten years after the fall of communism, most streets in Odessa are still – or again – known by two names. Visitors who last came to the city on the Black Sea twenty or thirty years ago may find it quite difficult to get their bearings. Is Ekaterin Street the street formerly known as Karl-Marx-Street or Lenin Street, and what may Langeron Street have once been called? But this difficulty is quickly surmounted, since the grid structure mentioned earlier and the numbering of the houses – getting lower toward the sea end, with the even numbers always on one, the uneven numbers on the other side – is a great help in navigating through the city. In spite of all the confusion about names, in the case of one street there is no problem whatsoever: Deribasovskaya.

This is by no means the most beautiful street in Odessa, it is not lined with the plane trees typical of the city or white acacias, and it can't boast any of the oldest or grandest buildings, theatres or smart hotels.

But the Deribasovskaya is to Odessa what the Kurfürstendamm is to Berlin, the Oxford Street is to London or the Champs Elysées is to Paris. The street has always been known as Deribasovskaya – through all periods of history. This is quite something, as the street was named after the staunchly tsarist officer José de Ribas, conqueror of the Turkish fortress of Khadzhi-Bej. But even the Soviets did not dare to make a change here.

What then makes this street so special? Above all, the people. For the last few years, public traffic has been banned from Deribasovskaya, so that it is no longer necessary to push through the crowd on the eleven meter wide pavements when showing off the newest fashion, hurrying to an appointment or wandering along deep in thought.

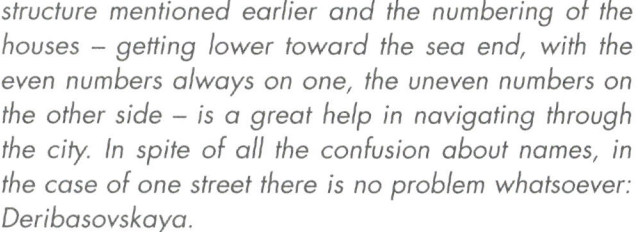

Aber die Deribassowskaja ist für Odessa das, was für Berlin der Kudamm, für London die Oxford Street oder Paris die Champs Elysée sind. Die Deribassowskaja war immer die Deribassowskaja – zu allen Zeiten. Das bedeutet schon immerhin etwas, denn der Namensgeber war kein geringerer als der zaristische Offizier José de Ribas, der Eroberer der Türkenfestung Hadshibej. Selbst die sowjetische Ära konnte daran nicht rütteln.

Was macht nun das Flair dieser Straße aus? Es sind vor allem die Menschen. Seit vor ein paar Jahren der öffentliche Verkehr auf der Deribassowskaja untersagt wurde, muss man sich nicht mehr auf den elf Meter breiten Gehwegen aneinander vorbei zwängen, um sich zu präsentieren, vorwärts zu eilen oder einfach nur sinnend daher zu schlendern.

Die Deribassowskaja ist nicht so lang wie ihre prominenten Pendants in Europa, lediglich 1082 Schritte ergab ein abschätzender Spaziergang zu früher Morgenstunde, denn nur zu dieser Zeit ist sie so leer, dass man die gesamte Länge möglichst gerade abschreiten kann, tagsüber geht das nur im Zickzack. Am oberen Ende – die Straße ist leicht abschüssig – beginnt die Deribassowskaja an der Kreuzung zur Preobrashenskaja Straße, früher Straße der Sowjetarmee. Diese führt übrigens in Richtung Meer in den ältesten Teil der Stadt – zur Gogolstraße. Der berühmte Dichter war zu allen Zeiten ‚politisch korrekt', so dass auch die Gogolstraße in der Sowjetunion nicht umbenannt wurde.

Bevor man in die Deribassowskaja eintaucht, lohnt sich ein Blick von der anderen Straßenseite. Dazu muss man die Preobrashenskaja überwinden. Das ist nicht ganz so einfach, denn die Autos rollen Stoßstange an Stoßstange. Und hat man rechter Hand an einer Ampel Rot, ist links garantiert Grün. Übrigens, die vorwiegenden Modelle auf vier Rädern stammen aus Japan und Westeuropa, dazwischen zwängen sich noch die ‚Oldtimer' der Marken Lada und Wolga.

Deribasovskaya Street is not as long as its famous counterparts in Europe. On an early morning walk to test the length of the street it took us 1082 steps to cover the entire stretch, early morning being the only time of day when the street is sufficiently empty to be able to walk straight ahead, without constantly having to dodge on-coming pedestrians.

At the top end – the street is on a slight slope – Deribasovskaya begins at the crossroads with Preobrazhenskaya Street, formerly Soviet Army Street. Preobrazhenskaya Street, incidentally, leads down to the sea, towards the oldest part of town, Gogol Street. The famous poet has always been considered 'politically correct', so that Gogol Street also kept its name throughout the Soviet period.

Before entering the bustle of Deribasovskaya it is worth taking a look from the other side of the street. To do this it is necessary to cross Preobrazhenskaya Street. This is not all that easy, as the cars drive along it bumper to bumper. An added difficulty is the setting of the traffic lights, which usually turn green for vehicles coming from the left, just when they have finally turned red for those advancing from the right. The most common models of car, by the way, are Japanese or Western European, interspersed with the occasional vintage Lada or Volga.

Once the street has been successfully crossed – there is a pedestrian subway for the not-so-courageous – there is a wonderful view of the façade of the 'Passage' (pronounced as in French!): this is a large building incorporating a hotel, supermarket and many shops. The interior of the Hotel 'Passage' still exudes the charm of Soviet simplicity. Foreign, or, to be more precise, western tourists rarely stay here, as the address is not listed on the internet or in the guidebooks. Nevertheless, the architecture of the building and particularly the nineteenth century indoor shopping precinct are quite astonishing, although at the moment the view is somewhat obscured by the small kiosks and stalls that have been erected. These, however, will probably disappear at some point.

**Erinnerungsfoto mit dem beliebten Komponisten
und Jazzsänger Leonid Utesov**
*Souvenir photograph featuring the popular composer
and jazz singer Leonid Utesov*

**Einer der „Zwölf Stühle" aus dem satirischen Roman
der Odessaer Schriftsteller Ilja Ilf und Jewgeni Petroff**
*One of the "Twelve Chairs" from the satirical novel
by the two Odessite writers Ilja Ilv and Jevgenij Petrov*

Die ,Passage': Einkaufszentrum und Hotel
in architektonischer Schönheit
*The 'Passage': shopping centre and hotel
in beautiful architectural style*

Hat man die Straße endlich überquert – der Vorsichtige kann auch eine Unterführung benutzen –, bietet sich ein herrlicher Blick auf die Fassaden der ‚Passage': Ein Gebäudekomplex mit Hotel, Supermarkt und vielen Geschäften. Das Hotel ‚Passage' besitzt im Inneren noch den Charme sowjetischer Einfachheit. Ausländische, korrekterweise müsste man sagen westliche Touristen steigen hier seltener ab, da es in den einschlägigen Reiseführern oder Internetadressen nicht gelistet ist. Dennoch, die Architektur und besonders die Innenpassage lassen den Betrachter erstaunen, auch wenn derzeit kleine Kioske und Verkaufsstände diese Ansicht beeinträchtigen. Das wird sicher nicht immer so bleiben.

Der Spaziergang auf der Deribassowskaja beginnt an der ‚Passage'. Auf der gegenüberliegenden Straßenseite, nach Juwelierläden und dem Restaurant ‚Woronzow', steht ein Stuhl aus Messing, ein Magnet für Erinnerungsfotos. Er ist ein besonderer, einer von zwölf Stühlen: Der satirische Roman „Zwölf Stühle" stammt aus der Feder der beiden Odessaer Schriftsteller Ilja Ilf und Jewgeni Petrow: Erzählt wird die Jagd nach einem Millionenschatz, der im Polster eines der Stühle versteckt ist. Dort hinein hatte eine Aristokratin aus Angst vor der Oktoberrevolution ihren wertvollen Schmuck genäht. Die Möbelstücke kommen bei einer Auktion unter den Hammer und werden in alle Himmelsrichtungen verstreut. Der Roman diente auch als Vorlage für den deutschen Spielfilm „Die dreizehn Stühle", in dem Heinz Rühmann und Hans Moser die Hauptrollen spielten.

An den Standort dieses Messingstuhls schließt sich der Stadtpark an. Hier befindet sich ein Kunstmarkt, von dem man allerdings nicht allzu viel erwarten sollte, dennoch kann man das eine oder andere Souvenir erstehen: Zeichnungen, Bilder, Schmuck, Kunsthandwerk, Mineralien – alles, was das Touristenherz erfreut. Über den Kunstmarkt sollte man auf alle Fälle schlendern, denn man trifft dort auf ein interessantes Völkchen von Händlern, Künstlern und Gauklern.

33

A walk down Deribasovskaya begins outside the 'Passage'. On the opposite side of the road, next to the jewellers shops and the restaurant 'Voronzov', stands a brass chair. This is a very popular spot for souvenir photographs. It is, of course, a very particular chair, one of a set of twelve: the satirical novel "Twelve Chairs" was written by the two Odessite writers Ilja Ilv and Jevgenij Petrov. The book tells the story of a treasure hunt for a fortune hidden in the upholstered seat of one of the chairs. The treasure, consisting of jewellery, is inserted into the seat by a lady of the aristocracy, trying to save her gems from the Russian Revolution. The twelve chairs however end up being sold at auction and scattered all over the country, without a record of which contains the treasure. Amongst others, the German film "The Thirteen Chairs", in which Heinz Rühmann and Hans Moser play the lead roles, was based on the novel.

The brass chair stands on the corner of the city gardens. In the gardens is an arts and crafts market where some quite pleasant souvenirs are sold, though the general standard is not very high. Sketches, paintings, jewellery, minerals and craftwork, all aimed at the tourist market, are on sale. A walk across the market is nevertheless worthwhile because of the interesting people who hang out there.

Opposite, on the corner of Vice-Admiral-Zhukov-Street, there is a vaulted cellar, home to a traditional pub and beer house, the 'Gambrinus'. The pub stays pleasantly cool even on hot summer days when temperatures in the street rise above 30°C. The cellar is somewhat dingy, the beer is no better than elsewhere, but a little more expensive, and somehow the mood at the long wooden tables of the pub is rarely truly cosy or relaxed.

**Musik gehört zur Deribassowskaja:
Ob klassisch oder folkloristisch, von Profis
oder Laien.**
*Music of all kinds is at home
on Deribasovskaya, be it classical or folk,
performed by professionals and amateurs.*

Der Kunstmarkt lockt besonders Touristen an.
The arts and crafts market mainly attracts the tourists.

Etwas abseits der Deribassowskaja: Der Buch- und CD-Markt
A short distance from Deribasovskaya: the book and CD market

Gegenüber, an der Ecke zur Vizeadmiral-Shukow-Straße, befindet sich in einem Kellergewölbe die traditionelle Biergaststätte ‚Gambrinus'. Hier ist es auch an heißeren Sommertagen angenehm kühl, wenn draußen die 30°C im Schatten überschritten sind. In dem Steingewölbe ist es schummrig, das Bier ist nicht besser als anderswo, dafür aber etwas teurer, und irgendwie will an den langen Holztischen nur schwer Gemütlichkeit aufkommen.

Wieder oben, lohnt sich ein Blick nach rechts auf den Griechischen Platz (Martinowskiplatz), seit eh und je ein zentraler Handelsplatz. Hier befindet sich u.a. ein großer Buch-, Software- und CD-Markt, auf dem fast jeder Titel preiswert zu bekommen ist – als Plagiat, versteht sich.

Gegenüber des ‚Gambrinus' steht – verhüllt durch Baugerüste und Abdeckfolien – das traditionelle Hotel ‚Moskau'. Das Gebäude ist eines der vielen Objekte, die unter der Obhut der obersten Denkmalschutzbehörde stehen. Daher bewirbt sich die Stadt Odessa auch bei der UNESCO um die Aufnahme des historischen Zentrums als Weltkulturerbe.

Back on the street, a short detour to the right is indicated, to visit Greek Square (formerly Martinovsky Square) which has always been the location of one of Odessa's central markets. Amongst others there is a large market trading in compact discs, computer software and books, where practically every item is on offer at a bargain price – in the form of a pirate copy, of course.

Opposite the 'Gambrinus' is Hotel 'Moscow', which has a great tradition, but at present is shrouded in scaffolding and plastic sheeting. The building is one of the many which are listed as being part of the national heritage. In view of the many historic buildings, the city has launched a bid to have the historic centre declared a UNESCO world heritage site.

Further along Deribasovskaya a gentle stroll, with an occasional change of sides, will take you past a mixture of shops and restaurants: boutiques, a book store, jewellery shops, the Irish pub 'Mc O'Neill' next to the 'Fidel' and 'McDonalds' and, only a couple of yards on, the 'Lakomka' ('sweet tooth'), a restaurant specialising in traditional Ukrainian fare, all face on to the street.

Gemütlich geht es weiter auf der Deribassowskaja, mal auf der einen, mal auf der anderen Straßenseite. Geschäfte und Restaurants wechseln sich ab: Boutiquen, ein Buchladen, Juweliergeschäfte, der Irish Pub 'Mc O'Neil' neben dem 'Fidel' und 'McDonalds', nur zwanzig Schritte weiter das 'Lakomka' ('Naschkatze') – eine Gaststätte für ukrainische Spezialitäten.

Ein Wort zu den Restaurants. Die Küche ist gut, die Preise für den Westeuropäer verlockend. Für weniger als zehn Euro erhält man schon ein Drei-Gänge-Menü, ein Glas Wein inklusive. Allerdings muss man einiges beachten, denn es gibt so manche Preisfalle. Bestellt man zum Essen beispielsweise Bier oder Wein, ohne speziell die Sorte zu nennen, erhält man mit großer Sicherheit ein Importprodukt. Das ist dann mindestens doppelt so teuer wie ein Einheimisches und nicht unbedingt besser. Wer die Sprache nicht beherrscht, sollte auf jeden Fall ein Lexikon dabei haben. Nur in den gehobenen Restaurants gibt es einen englischsprachigen Teil in der Speisekarte. Das Beste also ist, man kann etwas russisch sprechen oder hat einen Dolmetscher dabei. Bei Bier oder Wein reicht es schon aus, „mjestnoje pivo" oder „mjestnoje vino" zu bestellen, um ein einheimisches Produkt zu bekommen. Trauen Sie sich!

Ohne Geld geht auch in Odessa gar nichts. Die ukrainische Währung heißt Griwna; Euro oder Dollar können problemlos in den zahlreichen Bankfilialen gewechselt werden. Die Kurse unterscheiden sich von Haus zu Haus nur sehr gering. In fast allen Banken gibt es auch Geldautomaten, die die gängigen Kreditkarten wie American Express, Master-, Euro- oder Visa-Card akzeptieren. Typisch sind die vielen kleinen Wechselstuben – meist nur ein Fensterchen in einer Häuserfront – doch ein Papier mit rundem Stempel bescheinigt dem Besitzer, dass alles ganz legal ist.

Öffentlichen Straßenverkehr gibt es auf der Deribassowskaja nur an den Spielautomaten. *The only place where driving is permitted on Deribasovskaya are the slot machines.*

A brief comment on the topic of restaurants. The food is usually good, the prices are very attractive to Western Europeans. A three-coursemeal including a glass of wine is available for less than ten euros. There are however certain traps to watch out for where prices are concerned. For example, if guests order beer or wine with a meal, without specifying which sort, the waitress will automatically bring an imported brand which may not be any nicer than the local produce, but is guaranteed to be twice as expensive. Visitors who don't speak at least a little bit of Russian should definitely carry some sort of dictionary, as only the most expensive restaurants provide an English menu. The best bet is, of course, to either speak some Russian or take along someone to interpret. However, if you pluck up the courage and order "mjestnoe pivo" or "mjestnoe vino" you will also be served the local drinks!

38

Aus dem Straßenbild verschwunden sind allerdings die legendären Mineralwasserautomaten. Daher kann der Besucher heute diesen Genuss leider nicht mehr erleben, wie er in einem älteren Reiseführer beschrieben wurde: „Wie in den anderen Straßen, so sind auch in der Deribassowskaja Automaten für Selterwasser aufgestellt, die äußerlich entfernt an Telefonzellen erinnern, nur dass sie blau sind. Für eine Kopeke (ca. zwei Cent) erhält man ein Glas schmackhaftes Wasser, für drei Kopeken ein Glas Selters mit Sirupzusatz."

Auf der Deribassowskaja mit ihren 35 Metern Breite trifft man auf interessante Zeitgenossen. Viele verdienen sich hier ihren Lebensunterhalt, wie z.B. ein junger Mann mit einer weißen Python. Für ein geringes Entgelt kann man sich mit der harmlosen ‚Bestie' fotografieren lassen.

Ein Erinnerungsfoto mit einer Harley-Davidson mitten auf der Deribassowskaja ist nicht jedermanns Geschmack, aber für Touristen aus Sibirien, dem Kaukasus oder aus Mittelasien ist eine Harley sicher eine Attraktion. Übrigens, recht ungewöhnlich ist, dass in Odessa kaum Motorräder oder Fahrräder im Straßenverkehr zu sehen sind, was bei den unzähligen Schlaglöchern kein Wunder ist. Dagegen kann das neueste Porsche-Modell schon am Tag nach seiner Deutschland-Premiere am Primorski Boulevard bestaunt werden.

Ein eigenes Leben auf der Deribassowskaja führen die Straßenmusikanten. Da erklingen russische Weisen und lateinamerikanischer Tango. Klassische Operntenöre und dilettantische Amateure geben für ein paar Kopeken ihr Bestes. Zum Straßenbild gehören aber auch die Bettler. Einige von ihnen sind aufdringliche Kinder, die auf der Straße geduldet, in den Restaurants allerdings vom Personal vertrieben werden.

Nicht selten zu beobachten sind Menschen, die Abfalltonnen nach noch irgend Brauchbarem durchwühlen. Ihr Anblick ruft Ekel und Mitleid zugleich hervor. Es sind zumeist Ältere, die nur eine winzige Rente erhalten. Sie sind die Ärmsten der Gesellschaft.

Just like the world over, nothing works without cash in Odessa. The Ukrainian currency is called grivna, euros and dollars can be exchanged in the many banks without any trouble at all. The exchange rates hardly differ from bank to bank. Most banks also have cash points which accept the major credit cards such as American Express, Master, Euro or Visa. The large number of tiny money exchange shops – often no more than a little window in the front of a building – is typical of Odessa, a piece of paper with a round stamp however is proof of the fact that the transactions made by these little enterprises are completely legal.

The legendary soda water machines on the other hand have disappeared from the streets. Visitors can therefore no longer sample this particular treat, described in an old guide book to the city, "Just as in other streets, there are soda machines in Deribasovskaya Street which are faintly reminiscent of telephone boxes, only that they are painted blue. Here, one kopeck (approx. 2 cents) will buy a glass of water which tastes very pleasant, three kopecks a glass of soda water flavoured with syrup."

Deribasovskaya Street, which is thirty five metres wide, is populated with an interesting mixture of people, many of whom earn a living along the thriving street. For example, there is a young man with a white python. In exchange for a small sum of money visitors can have their picture taken with the harmless 'monster'.

**Der Euro steht längst nicht mehr
im Schatten des Dollar.**
The euro no longer comes second to the dollar.

Having your photograph taken on a Harley-Davidson bike set up on the middle of Deribasovskaya may not be your idea of a tasteful souvenir, but for tourists from Siberia, the Caucasus or Central Asia, such a motorbike is quite an attraction. One unusual feature of Odessa, by the way, is the more or less complete lack of bicycles and motorbikes among the traffic on the roads which, on the other hand, may not be so surprising considering the large number of potholes. The newest model of Porsche, in contrast, tends to be on show on Primorsky Boulevard the day after its launch in Germany.

The buskers on Deribasovskaja lead a life all of their own. They perform everything from Russian folk tunes to Latin American tango. Classically trained tenors and complete amateurs make tremendous efforts to earn a couple of kopecks. Another constant feature of life on Deribasovskaja are the many beggars. Many of these are children who beg very persistently and are tolerated on the streets, but are turned out of the restaurants by the staff.

People searching for usable items in the rubbish bins are not an uncommon feature on the streets of Odessa, and the sight of these scroungers is both repellent and pityful. Usually, they are elderly people who receive only a tiny pension. They tend to be the poorest members of society.

At the crossroads of Deribasovskaya and Richelieu Street the visitor's attention is drawn almost automatically to the left. There, approximately one hundred metres away, stands the opera house, a most magnificent building. This is just the right point to leave Deribasovskaya and go in search of the cultural treasures in the historic city centre.

**Tummelplatz
für Geschäftstüchtige**
*A hotspot for
smart businessmen*

Folgt man weiter der Deribassowskaja bis zur Kreuzung Richelieustraße, wendet man automatisch den Blick nach links. In ungefähr hundert Metern Entfernung erhebt sich prunkvoll das Gebäude des Operntheaters. Dieser Prachtbau macht es einem leicht, die Deribassowskaja zu verlassen und die Suche nach den kulturellen Schätzen der historischen Altstadt zu beginnen.

Altstadt:
Auf Entdeckungstour im historischen Zentrum

The city centre:
a voyage of discovery through the historic areas of the town

Das Innere des Operntheaters:
Prunkvoll bis ins Detail
The interior of the opera house:
sumptuous down to the details

Das Operntheater hat im wahrsten Sinne des Wortes eine bewegte Geschichte. Das Haus befindet sich an der Stelle, wo die frühere Türkenfestung Hadshibej lag.

Bereits im Jahre 1810 wurde das erste Theater der Stadt mit immerhin schon 800 Plätzen eröffnet – davon im Parterre nur ganze 44 Sitzplätze, ansonsten genoss man die Kunst zu jener Zeit stehend. Das Gebäude brannte im Winter des Jahres 1873 nieder. Die Stadt rief die Bevölkerung zu Spenden auf, um einen Wiederaufbau zu finanzieren. Das brachte den Großteil des notwendigen Geldes für ein neues Theater ein. Wohl deshalb sind die Odessiten auch heute noch stolz auf ihr Opernhaus – und das zu Recht. Schon in der Mitte des 19. Jahrhunderts wollten die Odessaer Bürger nicht nur irgendein Theater. Die Stadt schrieb damals einen internationalen Wettbewerb aus, man plante „ein mit Gold überzogenes, mit zahlreichen Skulpturen geschmücktes und mit prächtigen Treppen versehenes Prunkstück, das seinesgleichen in der Welt suchte."

Der Entwurf der Wiener Architekten Hermann Helmer und Ferdinand Fellner erhielt den Zuschlag. In dreijähriger Bauzeit (1884–1887) entstand ein Theater, dessen Äußeres – eine Mischung aus italienischer Renaissance und französischem Rokoko – eine Einheit mit dem im Inneren dominierenden Barock bildet.

The opera house has had a very varied history. The building stands on the site once occupied by the Turkish fortress of Khadzhi-Bej. The city's first theatre was opened in 1810. It could accommodate a proud total of eight hundred theatre-goers – although there were only forty-four seats in the stalls, as it was more usual to stand for performances in those days. The building was destroyed by a fire in the winter of 1873. The city appealed to its citizens for donations to finance the rebuilding. The appeal succeeded in raising most of the required sum. This is probably the reason why Odessites are so proud – and rightfully so – of their opera house. The mid-nineteenth century Odessites were not satisfied with having just a basic theatre. Instead, the city launched an international competition; the plan was to build "a gem, covered in gold, decorated with a large number of sculptures and equipped with most generous staircases, to compete with the best opera houses in the world."

The design created by the Viennese architects Hermann Helmer and Ferdinand Fellner was selected. Within three years (1884–1887), a theatre was constructed which combines an exterior mixing the Italian Renaissance and French Rococo styles with an interior which is predominantly reminiscent of the Baroque style.

Das Operntheater gilt weltweit als eines der schönsten Gebäude seiner Art und bietet 1600 Besuchern Platz.
The opera house is considered one of the most beautiful buildings of its kind in the world and can accommodate 1600 visitors.

**Vor dem Archäologischen Museum:
Kopie der berühmten Laokoon-Gruppe**
*The copy of the famous Laocoon group
outside the Archaeological Museum*

Wie so zahlreiche architektonische Perlen der Stadt, litt auch das Operntheater während der Sowjetzeit und noch nach der Perestroika unter der Vernachlässigung durch den Denkmalschutz. Erst seit Beginn des neuen Jahrtausends – es ist auch ein neuer Beginn für das Operntheater – ging man verstärkt an die Erhaltung dieses prunkvollen Gebäudes, und es war allerhöchste Zeit. Denn wie fast ganz Odessa ist auch das Gelände um das Operntheater von Katakomben unterhöhlt, was dazu führte, dass sich das Gebäude immer stärker absenkte. Betonpfähle sollen dem Operntheater nun einen dauerhaften Halt geben. Dazu wurden insgesamt 1800 Pfähle aus Stahlbeton bis auf eine Tiefe von 16 Metern in den Untergrund gerammt und miteinander verbunden. Das Fundament soll nun mindestens für die nächsten 100 Jahre halten.

Für die Innenrestaurierung wurden über 18 Kilogramm Blattgold verarbeitet und auch der Kronleuchter erstrahlt in neuem Glanz. Lediglich der 36 Tonnen schwere Bühnenvorhang aus rotem Samt und mehrere hundert Stühle warten noch auf ihre Erneuerung.

Die Saalakustik des Operntheaters ist exzellent und seine Künstler haben nicht nur in der Ukraine einen guten Ruf. Sie geben Konzerte und Gastspiele auf den Bühnen der ganzen Welt. Ein Gang durch das Gebäude gleicht einer Zeitreise durch die griechische Mythologie, sowie durch die russische und europäische Literatur. Skulpturen und Gemälde im Foyer, bei den Treppen, der Loge und der Balustrade faszinieren den Besucher auf Schritt und Tritt. Das ausverkaufte Haus fasst immerhin über 1600 Personen. Und noch eine Tatsache macht einen Besuch lohnenswert: Die Eintrittspreise sind für (west-)europäische Verhältnisse extrem attraktiv, um nicht zu sagen spottbillig.

Das Archäologische Museum ist das älteste der Museen von Odessa. *The Archaeological Museum is the oldest of Odessa's museums.*

Like many other architectural treasures around the city, the opera suffered a great deal from a lack of conservation work throughout the Soviet era and in the period immediately following Perestroika. The beginning of the new millennium has also brought a new lease of life for the opera house. Serious measures for the preservation of this great building are being undertaken, just in time. Like most of Odessa, the area around the opera house is undermined by a network of catacombs, and the building had begun to subside. In future, pillars of concrete will give the opera house permanent support. To achieve this, one thousand eight hundred interconnected pillars of reinforced concrete were inserted beneath the building, reaching down to a depth of sixteen metres below the foundations. The foundations are now supposed to be secure for at least the coming century.

In restoring the interior, more than eighteen kilograms of gold leaf were used and the chandelier was restored back to its former glory. Now, only the red velvet curtain, which weighs thirty-six tons, and several hundred seats are waiting to be replaced.

In weniger als fünf Minuten zu Fuß gelangt man vom Operntheater zum beliebten Primorski Boulevard. Es macht zu jeder Tageszeit Spaß, hier gemütlich entlang zu schlendern. Auf der kurzen Strecke kommt man an zahlreichen Denkmälern und Museen vorbei.

Vor dem Archäologischen Museum steht die Kopie der berühmten Laokoon-Gruppe. Das Original aus dem 1. Jahrhundert v. Chr. befindet sich heute im Vatikan. Das Archäologische Museum war das erste Museum von Odessa. Es wurde bereits im Jahre 1825 gegründet, da gab es die Stadt gerade einmal dreißig Jahre. Sein Eingang wird von vier korinthischen Säulen getragen. Das Museum selbst besitzt über 150.000 Exponate und ist mit seiner umfangreichen Sammlung alter Denkmäler und Fundstücke, die insbesondere aus dem Schwarzmeergebiet stammen, einzigartig. Lohnenswert ist aber auch ein Blick in die ‚Goldene Schatzkammer' oder in das ‚Ägyptische Kabinett'.

Wer sich für technische Details der alten und der modernen Seefahrt interessiert, wird im nahe gelegenen Schifffahrtsmuseum fündig. Das Gebäude wurde 1842 von dem Architekten G. Toricelli als ‚Englischer Club' errichtet und war anfänglich nur dem männlichen Teil der begüterten Einwohner zugänglich. Auch hier gibt es derzeit über 100.000 Ausstellungsstücke zu bewundern.

The accoustics of the theatre itself are excellent and the opera's musicians and singers are renowned across the Ukraine and beyond. They perform at concerts and guest performances all over the world. A tour of the building is like a journey through Greek mythology as well as Russian and European literature. Sculptures and paintings are arranged all around the entrance hall, along the staircases, the boxes and balustrade, vying for the theatre-goers' attention. When the house is sold out, there can be up to one thousand six hundred visitors. A further feature that makes a visit very worthwhile are the ticket prices which are very reasonable, not to say cheap, by (Western) European standards.

It is less than five minutes' walk from the opera house to the popular Primorsky Boulevard. A leisurely stroll along this street is good fun at any time of day. A large number of monuments and museums are situated along the short route. Outside the Archaeological Museum there is a copy of the famous Laocoon group. The original goes back to the first century before Christ and is now kept in the Vatican.

The Archaeological Museum was Odessa's first museum. It was opened in 1825, just thirty years after the founding of the city. The porch of the museum is supported by four Corinthian columns. The museum itself houses more than 150,000 pieces and its huge collection of ancient monuments and archaeological finds, mostly from the Black Sea region, is unique. Visits to the 'Golden Treasury' or the 'Egyptian Department' are also worthwhile.

The nearby Museum of Shipping supplies a host of technical details on maritime history and modern seafaring. The building was erected in 1842 by the architect G. Toricelli as an 'English Club' and was originally only open to the male section of the upper classes. This museum also has more than 100,000 pieces on show at the moment.

**Früher trafen sich die Reichen der Stadt
im ‚Englischen Club‘, heute befinden sich hier die über
100.000 Exponate des Schifffahrtsmuseums.**
*In the olden days, the city's rich congregated
at the 'English Club', now the more than 100,000 exhibits
of the shipping museum are on show here.*

**Das Literaturmuseum bietet
für Ausstellungen und Konzerte
ein attraktives Ambiente.**
*The Museum of Literature
provides an attractive backdrop
for exhibitions and concerts.*

Der ‚Goldene Saal'
des Literaturmuseums
The 'Golden Hall' at the
Museum of Literature

Das Literaturmuseum mit seinem ‚Goldenen Saal' ist nur einen Katzensprung entfernt. Das Haus birgt Sammlungen von Dichtern und Schriftstellern des zaristischen Russland sowie Werke aus der sowjetischen Zeit. Die Künstler waren Gäste der Stadt oder lebten eine gewisse Zeit in Odessa, wie Alexander Puschkin (1799–1837) in den Jahren 1823/24. Von ihm stammen auch die Zeilen: *„Ich lebte damals im staubigen Odessa. Der Himmel ist dort lange klar. Dort setzt ein reger Handel geschäftig seine Segel, ..."*

Ähnliche Verse könnten Tolstoi, Gogol, Babel, Ostrowski, Tschechow oder der bulgarische Nationaldichter Christo Botev geschrieben haben, um nur einige der berühmtesten zu nennen, die sich zeitweise in Odessa aufhielten.

„Egal wohin du willst, du bist in fünf Minuten da!", lautet ein geflügeltes Wort in Odessa. Vom Literaturmuseum zum Primorski Boulevard sind es sogar weniger. Primorski Boulevard heißt in der Übersetzung soviel wie ‚Der Boulevard, der sich beim Meer befindet'. Parallel zur tiefer gelegenen Uferstraße, ist er die beliebteste ‚Flaniermeile' der Odessiten. Neben dem Gebäude des Stadtrats wacht hier ein in Bronze gegossener Puschkin auf seinem Sockel. Daneben steht eine alte Kanone aus dem Krieg gegen die Türken – ein nettes Zusammentreffen, denn Kanone heißt im Russischen: ‚Puschka'. Jede halbe Stunde ertönt aus klirrenden Lautsprechern, die schon die Vorkriegszeit erlebt haben müssen, die Melodie *„Odessa, meine Heimatstadt"* aus der Operette *„Weiße Akazie"* von Isaak Dunajewski. Ein Dach aus Platanenkronen spendet Schatten, genau richtig beim Spaziergang in den heißen Sommermonaten. Die Bänke auf dem Primorski Boulevard sind meist belegt von älteren Leuten, Schulkindern oder Liebespaaren. Deren Blicke streifen die vielen Kräne und Schiffe, sie träumen vielleicht von fernen Orten oder denken an die Zeilen aus den Odessaer Erzählungen von Isaak Babel: *„In Odessa gibt es einen Hafen, und im Hafen liegen Dampfer aus Newcastle, Cardiff, Marseille und Port Said. Neger, Engländer, Franzosen und Amerikaner. Odessa kannte Zeiten der Blüte und es kennt Zeiten des Welkens, eines poetischen Vergehens, in dem ein Hauch Sorglosigkeit und sehr viel Hilflosigkeit liegen ..."*

Only a short walk away is the Museum of Literature which contains the 'Golden Hall'. The building is home to collections on the work of poets and writers of the tsars' era as well as the Soviet period. Most of them were guests of the city or lived in Odessa for a certain period of time, like Alexander Pushkin (1799–1837) in 1823 and 1824. On the subject of Odessa he wrote the verses, "Then, I lived in dusty Odessa. The sky stays bright there late and a lively trade sets its sails, ..."

Similar verses might have been written by Tolstoy, Gogol, Babel, Ostrovsky, Tshechov or the Bulgarian national poet Christo Botev, just some of the most famous writers to spend part of their lives in Odessa.

"Wherever you want to go, you will get there in five minutes!" is a popular saying in Odessa. The distance from the Museum of Literature to Primorsky Boulevard is even shorter. The English translation of the name Primorsky Boulevard is 'the Boulevard that runs along the seaside'. The Boulevard which is situated alongside the lower coast road is the Odessites' favourite place to hang out or go for leisurely walks. Close to the city council building a bronze statue of Pushkin keeps watch from its pedestal. Next to the statue stands an old canon, a leftover of the war against the Turks – an amusing combination, as the Russian word for canon is 'pushka'. Every half hour, the tune "Odessa, my home" from the operetta "White Acacia" by Isaac Dunajevsky is blasted from jarring loudspeakers which have probably been there since before the last war. A roof of plane trees provides shade, just right for a stroll during the hot summer months. The benches along Primorsky Boulevard are usually taken up by elderly people, school children and lovers. They gaze at the vista of ships and port machinery and perhaps dream of distant places or are reminded of the lines from Isaac Babel's Odessa Tales, "In Odessa there is a port, and ships from Newcastle, Cardiff, Marseille and Port Said are docked there. Negroes, Englishmen, Frenchmen and Americans. Odessa has known times when it has thrived, and times when it has wilted, a kind of poetic decline, which encompasses a touch of nonchalance and a lot of helplessness ..."

50

**Das legendäre Hotel ‚Londonskaja'
auf dem Primorski Boulevard**
*The legendary hotel 'Londonskaya'
on Primorsky Boulevard*

**Auf kommunistische Nostalgie
getrimmt: Das Restaurant ‚Déjà vu‘**
*The 'Déjà vu' restaurant caters to those
who feel nostalgic for communism.*

Natürlich könnte man den gesamten Boulevard in fünf Minuten abgehen, doch um die Atmosphäre auf sich wirken zu lassen, sollte man sich wesentlich mehr Zeit nehmen. Einer der bedeutenden Orte auf dem Primorski Boulevard ist das Hotel ‚Londonskaja', zur Zeit der Sowjetunion hieß es Hotel ‚Odessa'. Hier logierte im Jahre 1925 der Regisseur Sergej Eisenstein während der Dreharbeiten zu seinem berühmten Film „Panzerkreuzer Potemkin". Legendär und bekannt ist die Szene, in der ein Kinderwagen die ‚Potemkin'-Treppe herunterrollt, während das Militär auf die mit den meuternden Matrosen sympathisierende Bevölkerung schießt.

Der Namenspatron der Treppe war Grigori Alexandrovitsch Potemkin, Feldmarschall der zaristischen Armee und Liebhaber von Katharina II. Potemkin studierte an der Moskauer Universität und trat danach in den Armeedienst ein. Seine großen Erfolge hatte er zweifelsohne im Russisch-Türkischen Krieg und der Eroberung des Südens. Als andere seine Stelle als Liebhaber von Katharina II. einnahmen, blieb er jedoch einer ihrer engsten Berater.

Of course it is possible to walk down the entire Boulevard in five minutes, but a lot more time is necessary to take in the special atmosphere of the place. One of the important buildings along Primorsky Boulevard is the Hotel 'Londonskaya' which was called Hotel 'Odessa' during Soviet times. The director Sergej Eisenstein stayed here in 1925 while directing the making of his famous film "The Battleship Potemkin". The scene from the film in which a pram rolls down the famous 'Potemkin' Stairway while the military opens fire on civilians sympathising with the rebellious sailors has acquired cult status.

The stairway is named after Grigori Alexandrovich Potemkin, field marshal in the tsar's army and lover of Catherine II. Potemkin studied at Moscow University and then entered the military service. He was most successful during the Russian-Turkish war and the conquest of the south. Even after his place as the lover of Catherine II had been taken by others, he remained one of her most important advisors.

The 'Potemkin' Stairway is the symbol of the city of Odessa. It is also the connecting link between the historic part of the city and the port. The Stairway was erected in 1837–1841. Architecturally speaking, it is very cleverly designed: It consists of a total of one hundred and ninety-two steps and ten platforms. The bottom end is wider than the top and, due to the construction, viewed from the top the staircase appears to be a completely flat surface, while from the bottom only steps are visible. At the top end stands the 'Djuk' – the monument to Richelieu. From here, there is a fine view to be had of the harbour and the Morvoksal, the maritime train station. The panorama shows another of Odessa's contradictions: On a site which for many years was occupied by a small cocktail bar frequented by "sailors, students, whores and other lonely hearts", the largest hotel in Odessa has appeared. It was opened in 2000, with the name of the well-known international 'Kempinski' hotel chain blazoned across its front. But the management soon hit stormy waters. The hotel changed hands rapidly and so did the name. The inscription now visible from far off is 'Odessa'.

Der ‚Meeresbahnhof‘ ist der Passagierhafen von Odessa,
Blickfang für reizvolle Fotomotive. Vor einigen Jahren
wurde hier das weithin sichtbare Hotel ‚Odessa‘ errichtet.
*The maritime station 'Morvoksal' is the passenger port
of Odessa, a popular subject for photographers. A few years
ago the prominent 'Odessa' hotel was erected here.*

**Architektonisch raffiniert:
Die ‚Potemkin'-Treppe mit ihren 192 Stufen**
*A feat of architectural mastery:
the 192 steps of the 'Potemkin' Stairway*

Das ‚Haus der Wissenschaftler' ist eines der wenigen historisch wertvollen Gebäude, das in seiner Bausubstanz gut erhalten ist.
The 'House of the Scientists' is one of the few buildings of architectural importance which are in a good structural condition.

So wie an dem einen Ende das klassizistische Gebäude der früheren Kaufmannsbörse den Primorski Boulevard ziert, so befindet sich am anderen Ende das nicht minder berühmte, aber stark sanierungsbedürftige Schloss des Grafen Woronzow. Auch dieses Gebäude kennt verschiedene Besitzer. Die Grafenfamilie musste nach der Oktoberrevolution von 1917 den Deputierten der Arbeiter- und Matrosenräte weichen. In einem alten Reiseführer steht: *„Der Palast des Grafen Woronzow wurde im Jahre 1936 den Pionieren zur Verfügung gestellt. Sie erfüllten den ganzen Palast mit einer Atmosphäre der Freude, des Wissensdurstes und Schöpfertums …"*

Im Jahre 2003 steht das Haus immer noch leer, dringende Restaurierungsarbeiten gehen, wenn überhaupt, sehr zögerlich voran. Schilder warnen vor Einsturzgefahr. Mit der Aufnahme des historischen Zentrums von Odessa in die UNESCO-Liste des Weltkulturerbes wird zwar geliebäugelt, doch so lange darf nicht mehr gewartet werden. Wenn nichts getan wird, erlebt das ‚Woronzow'-Schloss die nächsten zehn Jahre nicht mehr. Hilfe könnte von „ganz oben" kommen. Die Internetseite www.odessaglobe.com berichtete von Plänen, aus dem maroden Fürstenschloss eine noble Staatsresidenz des amtierenden ukrainischen Präsidenten Leonid Kutschma zu machen.

Die ‚Potemkin'-Treppe: Erbaut in den Jahren 1837–1841 ist sie das Wahrzeichen der Stadt. Sie ist das Bindeglied zwischen dem Hafen und dem historischen Teil der Stadt und besitzt zahlreiche architektonische Raffinessen: Insgesamt besteht die ‚Potemkin'-Treppe aus 192 Stufen und zehn Absätzen. Am unteren Ende ist sie breiter als am oberen und so konstruiert, dass der Betrachter von oben nur ein geradliniges Plateau und von unten nur Treppenstufen sieht. Oben steht der ‚Djuk' – das Richelieu-Denkmal. Von hier hat man einen guten Blick über die Hafenanlagen und den ‚Morvoksal', den ‚Meeresbahnhof'. Das Panorama bietet dem Betrachter einen neuen Kontrast. An einer Stelle, an der eh und je eine kleine Cocktailbar stand, in der *„Matrosen, Studenten, Prostituierte und andere einsame Herzen"* ihre Zeit vertrieben, erhebt sich das größte Hotel in Odessa. Eröffnet im Jahre 2000 mit dem weithin sichtbaren Namenszug der international renommierten Hotelkette ‚Kempinski', kam das Management jedoch in unruhiges Fahrwasser. Die Eigentümer wechselten schnell und so auch der Name: Heute weithin sichtbar ist es nun das Hotel ‚Odessa'.

Viele Prachtfassaden bedürfen einer dringenden Restaurierung.
Many of the grand facades are in urgent need of repair.

The counterpart of the former stock market, whose magnificent building in the classicist style stands at one end of Primorsky Boulevard, is the palace of Duke Voronzov at the other end, a building no less famous, but in sad need of repair. This building has also known a long line of owners. The duke's family had to make room for the deputies of the workers' and sailors' soviets after the October revolution in 1917. An old guidebook reads, "The palace of Duke Voronzov was given to the young pioneers in 1936. They filled the whole palace with an atmosphere of joy, thirst for knowledge and creativity …"

In 2003 the building is still empty, urgent conservation work is progressing very slowly, if at all. Signs warn that the building is in danger of collapsing. Odessa may be hoping for its town centre to be registered as a UNESCO world heritage site, the repairs on the building should however not be left till this has been accomplished. If something is not done soon, the palace will not survive the coming decade. But help from "high places" may be close at hand. The internet site www.odessaglobe.com has reported on plans to turn the decrepit palace into an elegant state residence for the reigning Ukrainian president Leonid Kutchma.

Vom Verfall bedroht:
Die einst so attraktiven Hinterhöfe der Altstadt
Threatened with ruin:
the once so attractive courtyards
in the historic centre

Rhythmisches Springen kann die ,Schwiegermutterbrücke' in Schwingung versetzen.
Jumping up and down can make the 'mother-in-law bridge' sway.

Wird das ehemalige Schloss des Grafen Woronzow zur Residenz des ukrainischen Präsidenten?
Is the palace of Duke Voronzov destined to become the residence of the Ukrainian president?

60

Das Kunstmuseum birgt einen der wenigen Zugänge zu den Katakomben.
The Museum of Art contains one of the few entrances to the catacombs.

Vom Schloss aus führt eine Brücke in den ältesten Teil der Stadt. Im Volksmund heißt sie ‚Schwiegermutterbrücke'. Einen offiziellen Namen gibt es wohl auch nicht, zumindest kennt ihn niemand, wenn man fragt. Weitläufig bekannt ist jedoch die Legende um den Namen ‚Schwiegermutter': In den 60-er Jahren des 20. Jahrhunderts regierte in Odessa ein Bürgermeister, der mit seiner Frau und der Schwiegermutter jenseits einer kleinen Schlucht wohnte. Und da er vom Stadtrat aus immer nach Hause ging, wo seine Schwiegermutter das Mittagessen bereitete, wurde ihm der Weg runter und wieder hoch – und das dann auch noch mit vollem Bauch – einfach lästig. Deshalb gab er schließlich die Anweisung, eine Brücke zu bauen.

Die Brücke hat die Eigenschaft, stark im Winde zu schwingen. Wenn es an starkem Wind fehlt, machen sich insbesondere junge Leute das Vergnügen, durch rhythmisches Springen die Brücke in Schwingung zu versetzen und somit manchen älteren Mitbürger aufzuregen.

From the palace, a bridge leads to the oldest part of the city. The bridge is popularly known as the 'mother-in-law bridge'. An official name does not seem to exist, at any rate no one we asked could tell us one. The 'mother-in-law legend' on the other hand is widely known: In the 60's of the twentieth century, Odessa was governed by a mayor who, along with his wife and mother-in-law, lived on the other side of the small ravine that runs through that part of town. Since he had the habit of walking home from the town council every day to eat a lunch prepared by his mother-in-law, he soon tired of walking down the hill and up the other side – particularly after lunch, when his belly was full. He therefore gave instructions for a bridge to be built.

The bridge has a tendency to sway in the wind. When there are no high winds, the younger generation of Odessites particularly takes pleasure in jumping up and down rhythmically to make the bridge wobble and disconcert older members of the population.

From the 'mother-in-law bridge' a small 'fortress' comes into view at the end of Gogol Street. This 'fortress' has just been restored and is known as the Shah's palace. The building once belonged to the Shah of Persia, who fled the revolution in Iran (1905–1906) and took up residence in exile in Odessa. After the revolution of 1917 the palace was used by various state institutions, the condition of the building deteriorating steadily throughout the Soviet era.

One of the largest financial enterprises in the Ukraine, the 'Marine Transport Bank', has now set up its central offices here. New legal rules make it possible for listed buildings to be restored by private enterprises. In return, these firms are given long-term leases on the properties at particularly attractive rates.

Im Kunstmuseum werden Exponate gut bewacht.
The exhibits at the Museum of Art are well looked after.

Zeitvertreib
im Kunst-
museum
*Pastime
at the Museum
of Art*

Von der ‚Schwiegermutterbrücke'
aus erblickt man eine kleine ‚Festung' am Ende der Gogolstraße.
Diese ‚Festung' ist neu restauriert
und wird als Schahpalast bezeichnet. Das Gebäude gehörte einst
dem Schah von Persien, der vor der
Revolution im Iran (1905–06) ins
Exil nach Odessa flüchtete. Nach
der Oktoberrevolution von 1917
wurde der Palast von verschiedenen staatlichen Einrichtungen ge-
nutzt, die Bausubstanz verfiel im Verlaufe der Sowjetzeit stetig. Eines der größten Finanzunternehmen in
der Ukraine, die ‚Schifffahrtsbank', hat heute hier seine
Zentrale. Neue gesetzliche Bestimmungen erlauben es,
dass Gebäude, die unter Denkmalschutz stehen, von
privaten Firmen restauriert werden. Sie erhalten im
Gegenzug langfristige Pachtverträge zu besonders
attraktiven Konditionen.

In der Gogolstraße befinden sich sehr alte und
architektonisch interessante Häuser. Das in der Straße
nachweislich älteste ist das Haus Nummer 8. Es wurde
in den 20-er Jahren des 19. Jahrhunderts von einem
unbekannten Architekten im Stil des russischen Empire
gebaut. Sehr auffällig ist das Gebäude gegenüber.
Zwei Atlanten, gebeugt von ihrer Last, tragen auf dem
Rücken einen Erdball, der wiederum als Stütze für den
sich darüber befindlichen Balkon dient. In diesem
Haus wohnte bis zur Übernahme der Macht durch die
Kommunisten im Jahre 1920 die deutsche Familie Falz-
Fein, reiche Handelsleute, die zu jener Zeit in weiten
Teilen der Ukraine und Russlands bekannt waren. Sie
flüchteten 1920 mit einem der letzten Schiffe nach
Westeuropa.

Die letzte Station des Altstadtbummels ist das
Kunstmuseum. Ursprünglich war es das Schloss des
Grafen Potocki, erbaut bereits in den Jahren 1805–
1810, zu einer Zeit also, da Odessa buchstäblich
noch in den Kinderschuhen steckte. Auch dieses zwei-
geschossige Gebäude ist eine Perle der Architektur.

**Das ‚Atlanten-
haus' in der
Gogolstraße**
*The Falz-Fein
residence in
Gogol Street*

*The houses on Gogol Street are
among the oldest in Odessa.
Number Eight is recorded as being
the oldest on street. It was built by
an unknown architect in the 20's of
the nineteenth century in the Russian Empire style. The house opposite is very striking. Two sculptures
of bearded male figures, bent
double with the weight, carry on
their backs the globe which in turn
supports the balcony above. This
house was home to the German
Falz-Fein family until 1920, when
the communists took power. The
family were rich merchants who at
the time were well known all over
large areas of Ukraine and Russia.
They fled Odessa for Western
Europe on one of the last ships to
leave the port.*

*The last stop on the tour of the
city centre is the Museum of Art.
Originally this was the palace of
Count Potocki, built in 1805–
1810, at a time when Odessa was
in its earliest youth. The two-story
building is another outstanding
example of Odessite architecture.*

Der Haupteingang befindet sich hinter einem aus sechs Säulen bestehenden Portikus. Ornamente und Stuckverzierungen schmücken die Fassade. Die Innenräume sind mit kunstvollen Deckenbemalungen, ornamentalen Verzierungen und kostbaren Parkettfußböden versehen. Die zahlreichen Ausstellungsräume zeigen Kunstwerke der berühmtesten russischen und ukrainischen Maler.

Eine vollkommen andersartige Attraktion des Gebäudes befindet sich zwei Etagen tiefer. Dort liegt einer der wenigen öffentlichen Zugänge zu den Katakomben. Bauleute in Odessa benutzten den unterirdisch gewonnenen Muschelkalkstein für den Hausbau. Dieses Material lässt sich leicht bearbeiten, ist schall- und wärmeisolierend, dafür aber sehr porös. Deshalb baute man in der Altstadt nur zwei- und dreigeschossige Häuser. Der Muschelkalkstein wurde fast 200 Jahre lang völlig unkontrolliert abgebaut. Es entstand ein Labyrinth aus Höhlen und Gängen – die Katakomben. Die gesamte Stadt ist unterhöhlt und daher kommt es ab und zu vor, dass ein Gebäude einfach absackt. Insgesamt sind es über 2000 Kilometer unterirdischer Wege, tödlich für jeden, der sich darin verirrt.

„Es herrscht absolute Dunkelheit. Bereits nach wenigen Minuten kann man sich nicht mehr orientieren, bekommt Angst- und Wahnzustände und verliert jeden Bezug zur Realität. Schmuggler nutzten die Katakomben als Versteck, reiche Familien für die Weinlagerung und so mancher Rivale verschwand dort auf nimmer Wiedersehen. Hierfür legte man spezielle Gruben an", wird bei Führungen durch die Katakomben gern von den Mitarbeitern des Kunstmuseums erzählt.

Die größte Bedeutung erlangten die Katakomben allerdings im Jahre 1941, als Odessa von deutschen und rumänischen Truppen besetzt wurde. Die unterirdischen Gänge waren für die Partisanen das einzig mögliche Versteck weit und breit: Gut organisiert, aber mit großen Versorgungs- und Ernährungsproblemen, überstanden sie so die Zeit der Okkupation. Als Ende 1943 auch Zivilpersonen in die Höhlen flüchteten, hielten sich zeitweise bis zu 10.000 Menschen in den Katakomben auf.

The main entrance is behind a portico consisting of six columns. Ornaments and stucco decorations adorn the façade. The rooms in the interior are equipped with ceiling paintings of the highest quality, ornamental decorations and valuable parquet floorings. The many rooms of the exhibition contain paintings by some of the most famous Russian and Ukrainian painters.

A completely different attraction of the building lies two stories below. Here, there is one of the few public entrances to the catacombs. Builders in Odessa used the limestone quarried underground to build houses. The stone is very easy to shape, insulates well against the cold and noise, but is very porous. This is the reason why only two and three-store houses were erected in the old city. The limestone was quarried for around two hundred years without any sort of supervision. A labyrinth of caves and passageways was created, the catacombs. The entire city is built on a system of burrows and in consequence, buildings occasionally suddenly subside. There is a total of two thousand kilometres of passage, lethal for anybody losing their way in the web.

"It is pitch dark down there. A person alone in the catacombs will loose his bearings completely in as little as a few minutes, develop paranoid conditions and lose all sense of reality. Smugglers used to use the catacombs as a hide-out, rich families as a wine-cellar and many rivals disappeared for good in the maze. For this purpose, special pits were constructed", the staff of the Museum of Art enjoy telling visitors on guided tours of the catacombs.

The catacombs however gained their greatest importance in 1941, when Odessa was occupied by German and Rumanian troops. The underground passages where the only possible hiding place far and wide for the partisans. Well organised, but with great difficulties concerning food supplies, they managed to survive the occupation. At times, when civilians started to seek shelter in the caves at the end of 1943, there were up to ten thousand people under ground in the catacombs.

Nachtleben:
Die Stadt schläft erst am Morgen ein

Nightlife:
The city rarely sleeps

**Hotel ‚Odessa':
Zahlreiche Gelegenheiten für
abendliches Amusement**
*The 'Odessa' hotel:
many options for an evening's
amusement*

Nachts sind alle Katzen grau. Das ist in Odessa nicht viel anders. Doch Katzen sieht man kaum, eher umherstreunende Hunde. Und noch eines bewirkt die Dunkelheit: Sie verdeckt die Kontraste! Im Schein der illuminierten Schaufenster, der hell erleuchteten Restaurants und in den Spotlights der Diskotheken, Spielsalons oder Nachtclubs bekommt alles Sichtbare ein elegantes Antlitz.

Natürlich besitzen die besten Hotels der Stadt die entsprechenden Einrichtungen, in denen man sich auch am späten Abend die Zeit vertreiben kann: Bar, Restaurant, Fitnessclub, Spielsalon, Kosmetik- und Wellnessabteilung.

Das einzige Fünf-Sterne-Hotel der Stadt ist das ‚Odessa' am Hafen. Hier zu nächtigen kann sich nicht jeder leisten. Von der gegenüberliegenden ‚Potemkin'-Treppe hat man einen hervorragenden Blick auf das eindrucksvolle Panorama: Der alte ‚Meeresbahnhof' aus den 60-ern des vorigen Jahrhunderts, dahinter das helle Hotelgebäude mit rotem Namenszug, die gelben Kräne und das Dunkel des Schwarzen Meeres.

Just like all over the world, Odessa bar-flies are attracted by the bright city lights. However, where the nightlife is concerned, there are no flies on Odessa!

For one thing, the darkness covers up many of the city's contradictions. In the light of the illuminated shop windows, the brightly lit restaurants and in the spotlights of the dance halls, casinos and nightclubs everything visible appears elegant and sleek.

Of course, the top hotels of the city offer all the amenities necessary to make the time after nightfall pleasant: bars, restaurants, gyms, casinos, beauty- and wellness areas.

The only five-star hotel is the 'Odessa' by the harbour. Not everyone can afford to stay there. From the 'Potemkin' stairway opposite, however, there is also a very good view of the magnificent panorama: the old 'maritime station', built in the 60's of the last century, behind it the pale building of the hotel with its red lettering, the yellow cranes in the port and the dark of the Black Sea.

Many visitors, but also the people of Odessa, enjoy going for a gentle stroll in the late evening. Primorsky Boulevard and its vicinity are ideal for walking out. The crime rate is no higher in Odessa than in Berlin or New York, nevertheless it is not particularly advisable for strangers to the city to wander too far from the centre at night. Apart from everything else, it is far more difficult to spot those dangerous man-hole covers in the poorly lit side streets!

Particularly in the warm months between May and September, the crowds are drawn to the streets and restaurants in the city centre. The wealthy show off their beauty – or their beautiful companions – on Deribasovskaya. Young ladies, claiming to be housewives, seek the acquaintance of wealthy gentlemen. Friends sit together in the street cafés.

Film buffs need to get used to the Russian custom of showing films dubbed with one single voice speaking all the parts and the original sound track audible in the background. It is probably preferable to go to a restaurant, nightclub or variety show! One of the best venues is the variety club 'Amsterdam', only five minutes from Deribasovskaya, of course. Dancing, singing, music and entertainment are on offer there every day, or rather every night.

Ob Disko oder Varieté:
Feiern bis zum Morgengrauen
Partying goes on till daybreak
both at the clubs and the
variety theatres.

Spielsalons werden streng bewacht.
Casinos are heavily guarded.

Nächtliche Stadt-Impressionen
Impressions of the nocturnal city

**Clubs auch für Homosexuelle:
Das etwas andere Nachtleben ist erst seit wenigen Jahren in Odessa möglich.**
*The advent of the gay bar:
Night life of this type has only recently become possible in Odessa.*

Getränkeverkauf am Straßenkiosk rund um die Uhr
Round the clock service at one of the street kiosks

Viele Besucher, aber auch Einheimische, nutzen die späten Abendstunden für einen geruhsamen Spaziergang. Dazu bieten gerade der Primorski Boulevard und seine nähere Umgebung beste Gelegenheit.

Die Kriminalität ist in Odessa zwar nicht höher als in Berlin oder New York, dennoch sollte man sich als Ortsunkundiger in der Nacht nicht allzu weit vom Zentrum entfernen. Außerdem sind in den spärlich beleuchteten Nebenstraßen die gefährlichen Gullydeckel schlecht zu sehen!

Gerade in den wärmeren Monaten von Mai bis September zieht es viele Menschen in die Straßen und Restaurants des Zentrums. Man flaniert auf der Deribassowskaja, um sich in seiner Schönheit oder mit seiner Schönen zu zeigen. Junge Damen, die sich als Hausfrauen ausgeben, suchen die Bekanntschaft zahlungsfähiger Männer. Man sitzt mit Freunden im Straßencafé. Wer gern ins Kino gehen möchte, muss sich daran gewöhnen, dass ausländische Filme zwar im Originalton laufen, aber meist nur von einer Stimme russisch übersprochen werden.

Dann lieber doch ins Restaurant, den Nachtclub oder das Varieté! Eine der ersten Adressen ist das Showtheater ‚Amsterdam' – natürlich nur fünf Minuten von der Deribassowskaja entfernt. Gesang, Tanz, Musik und Unterhaltung bis in die frühen Morgenstunden ist hier täglich – oder besser nächtlich – angesagt.

Etwas intimer geht es in einem kleinen Nachtclub in der Puschkinstraße zu. Er befindet sich versteckt in einem Keller und ist eher unter Insidern bekannt. Das Publikum hier ist jung, aber nicht jugendlich. Szenemusik und Tanzperformances werden geboten. Auch Schwule und Lesben können sich im Club unverhohlen zeigen, eine Tatsache, die zur Sowjetzeit kaum denkbar war – nicht einmal in Odessa.

Disco und Tanz gehen bis in die frühen Morgenstunden. Das ist eine Zeit, da meist ältere Menschen mit ihren Reisigbesen das Überflüssige der Nacht zusammenkehren und die Lastwagen mit ihren Wassertanks dem Straßenstaub den Kampf ansagen.

At a small nightclub on Pushkin Street the atmosphere is somewhat more intimate. It is situated in a basement and tends to be known only to insiders. The crowd here is young but not teen-age. The club offers up-to-the-minute music and dance-shows. Even gays and lesbians can be open about their preferences here, something which was unthinkable under the Soviet regime – even in Odessa.

Club-life and dancing goes on till the early hours of the morning. When the clubbers have gone home, another part of the population, mostly somewhat older, comes out with its brooms to clear away the debris of the night and lorries with tanks of water drive around the city, taking up the battle with the dust on the streets.

Ungewöhnliches Nachtquartier
Unusual sleeping quarters

**Morgenwäsche – trotz
Wassermangel im Sommer**
*Morning wash – in spite of
the summer drought*

Kunstsplitter:
Von der Muse wird man früh geküsst

Aspects of the arts:
Great artists need to start young

76 Malerei, Musik und Tanz haben eine lange Tradition in Odessa – in der Zarenzeit wie in den Jahren der Sowjetmacht. Die Vielfalt der Nationalitäten, die sich in der Stadt angesiedelt hatten, und das im doppelten Sinne angenehme Klima lockten immer wieder Künstler von nah und fern nach Odessa. Die Wurzeln der ‚Schönen Künste' sind auch heute nicht vertrocknet. Allerorts trifft man auf Liebhaber der Literatur, der modernen und klassischen Musik, ob zeichnende Kinder im Park oder malende Künstler in ihren Kellerateliers. Gerade in den letzten Jahren sind viele neue Galerien entstanden, sowohl staatlich geförderte als auch privat finanzierte.

Kunst kostet Geld, und Geld ist bekanntlich in Umbruchzeiten besonders knapp. ‚Finanzmittelbeschaffungskreativität' ist angesagt, falls nicht gerade die Eltern der zukünftigen Künstler betucht genug sind und sich einen Privatunterricht leisten können.

Bezeichnend für die neue Zeit ist die Entstehungsgeschichte der Rock-Oper „Romeo und Julia" des Odessaer Komponisten Wadim Lopejko. Über Fernsehen und lokale Presse suchte das Theater Jungen und Mädchen im Alter von 16 bis 22 Jahren für die Titelrollen. Es meldeten sich über eintausend Pärchen, und nach dem Casting betraten drei Julias und drei Romeos die Bretter, die die Welt bedeuten. Proben und Premiere im Theater der Musikalischen Komödie waren für sie ein Erfolg, auch wenn es nicht gleich auf die Bühne des berühmten Operntheaters ging.

Painting, music and dancing have a great history in Odessa and thrived under the tsars as well as in the Soviet days. The multitude of nationalities who had settled in the town and the pleasant climate, in the literal as well as the figurative sense of the word, in the city, drew artists from far and wide to Odessa. The 'beaux arts' are still doing well today. All over the place you will find lovers of literature, fans of classical and modern music, children sketching in the parks and artists working in their basement studios. The last few years particularly have seen the opening of a great number of new galleries, some with state support, some privately financed.

Art is expensive and it is well known that in times of social change there is usually a shortage of money. Creativity in tapping sources of possible finance is at a premium for those budding artists not blessed with wealthy parents capable of paying for private tuition.

The story of the creation of the rock-opera "Romeo and Juliet" by the Odessite composer Vadim Lopejko is typical of the new age. The theatre put out advertisements seeking young actors and actresses between sixteen and twenty-two years to play the lead roles. More than one thousand couples applied and after the auditions three Romeos and three Juliets stepped into the limelight. For these youngsters, making it through to the rehearsals and opening night at the Theatre of Musical Comedy has been a tremendous success-story, even if the doors to the famous opera house have not immediately opened to them.

**Anfänger und Profis bei der Probe
zur Rockoper „Romeo und Julia"**

*Beginners and professionals cooperate
in the rehearsals for "Romeo and Juliet".*

**„Mein Ziel? Die Schule abschließen,
eine Ballettausbildung und dann …
eine Profikarriere!"**

*"My goal? To finish school, train
as a ballet dancer and then … have
a professional career!"*

Harmonie: Schweizer Dirigent und ukrainischer Schüler
In harmony: a Swiss conductor with a Ukrainian pupil

Die Philharmonie: Erlebnis für Musikliebhaber
The Philharmonic: an experience for music lovers

Die Außenfassade der Musikalischen Komödie wirkt eher bescheiden. Das Gebäude entstand um 1970 in zweckorientierter, sowjetischer Bauart und ist bereits von innen und außen sanierungsbedürftig. Wirft man einen Blick in den Theaterraum und hinter die Kulissen, so hat man das Gefühl, die Zeit sei stehen geblieben. Die Bühnentechnik ist veraltet und für die Premiere von „Romeo und Julia" musste sich das Haus sogar eine Verstärkeranlage ausborgen. Kein Wunder, dass die Vorstellungen in der Musikalischen Komödie nicht zum Programm westeuropäischer Reiseunternehmen gehören. Dennoch, so meint der Rockmusiker und Komponist Lopejko, selbst Odessit in der dritten Generation: „Ich wollte meine moderne Rockoper über das ewige Thema ‚Romeo und Julia' unbedingt in Odessa inszenieren, hier wie kaum anderswo in der Ukraine bekommt man die Möglichkeit, eigene Sachen auszuprobieren; wo auf einer staatlichen Bühne nicht nur die Werke eines Offenbach, Verdi oder Strauß gegeben werden. Odessa bietet vielen einheimischen Künstlern und Nachwuchskräften ein Podest."

Manchmal kommt ein wenig Hilfe für junge Künstler ganz unverhofft und aus Richtungen, die bisher unüblich waren. Ein Beispiel ist die ‚Stoljarski'-Musikschule in Odessa. Seit dem Jahr 2000 wird sie vom Direktorium der Musikschule Konservatorium Bern unterstützt. Es werden gemeinsame Konzerte in der Schweiz und der Ukraine organisiert – da gibt es schon mal ein Cello oder ein anderes Instrument als Gastgeschenk. Derartige Aktivitäten zu organisieren und durchzuführen kostet ein gewisses Maß an Enthusiasmus und Stehvermögen. Allein die bürokratischen Probleme beim Zoll und anderen Einrichtungen, um ein Cello oder gar einen Flügel als Geschenk in die Ukraine einzuführen, sind nicht unerheblich.

The exterior of the Musical Comedy Theatre is comparatively modest. The building was erected in 1970 in the utilitarian Soviet style and is in need of repairs on both inside and the outside. In the stage area and behind the set the general feeling is that time has stopped. The stage machinery is old-fashioned and the theatre even had to borrow a sound system for the opening night of "Romeo and Juliet". No wonder that visits to the performances at the Musical Comedy Theatre are not part of the packages offered by Western European travel agencies. Nevertheless, the rock-musician and composer Lopejko, who is himself a third-generation Odessite, is adamant the city is the right place for his opera,

"I wanted to stage my modern rock-opera on the eternal topic of 'Romeo and Juliet' in Odessa and nowhere else. Nowhere in the Ukraine are people given the opportunity of trying out their own thing like they are in Odessa, where state theatres don't just perform the works of Offenbach, Verdi or Strauss. Odessa gives space to many local artists and newcomers."

Sometimes a little bit of help for young artists comes unexpectedly and from places hitherto unknown to the Odessa art world. The 'Stoljarsky' School of Music in Odessa is an example. Since 2000 it has been receiving the support of the head of the Bern Conservatory and School of Music. Joint concerts in Switzerland and Ukraine are carried out and occasionally a cello or other instrument arrives by way of a present to the hosts. Organising and carrying off projects such as these demands a certain amount of enthusiasm and steadfastness. The bureaucratic hurdles set up by the customs authorities when it comes to importing a cello or, worse still, a piano as a gift, are considerable.

Even more important than the presents however are the contacts established, according to Werner Schmitt, the head of Musikschule Conservatorium Bern, the academy of music in Bern in Switzerland. "We would like to keep up our friendship with the 'Stoljarsky' School of Music and if possible extend it. This is very important to me on a personal level, as it means that children from different cultures can get to know each other and play music together."

**Die ‚Stoljarski'-Musikschule:
Allgemeiner Schulunterricht und
musikalische Ausbildung in einem**
*The 'Stoljarsky' School of Music:
General schooling and musical education
rolled into one.*

82 Doch wichtiger als diese Geschenke sei der Kontakt, sagt Direktor Werner Schmitt aus Bern. *„Wir wollen unsere freundschaftlichen Beziehungen zur ‚Stoljarski'-Musikschule pflegen und erweitern. Das ist mir auch persönlich sehr wichtig, denn dieser Kontakt ermöglicht es, dass sich Kinder aus verschiedenen Kulturen begegnen und miteinander musizieren."*

Die ‚Stoljarski'-Schule blickt auf eine 70-jährige Tradition zurück. Ihr Begründer ist der Odessaer Geiger und Musikpädagoge Pjotr Solomonowitsch Stoljarski (1871–1944).

Die Schule brachte viele international bekannte Künstler hervor: Den Pianisten Boris Bloch, den Geiger Michail Weiman sowie den weltberühmten David Oistrach.

Gemeinsame Konzerte der jungen Musiker aus Odessa und Bern, zum Beispiel in der neu renovierten Odessaer Philharmonie, zählen zu den Höhepunkten der musikalischen Zusammenarbeit, als deren Ergebnis nicht selten Freundschaften unter den Kindern und Jugendlichen entstehen.

„Wahre Kunstwerke entstehen im Keller!", meint der talentierte Maler Konstantin Silen selbstbewusst. Er muss seine Werke nicht auf dem Kunstmarkt im Stadtpark anbieten. Der Maler verkauft das eine oder andere Bild während kleinerer Ausstellungen, erhält Aufträge von der Stadt oder im ‚nahen' Ausland wie Finnland oder Deutschland. Görlitz, Stuttgart und Tübingen waren bereits Orte seines Schaffens. Konstantin Silen studierte in Moskau Architektur, kam irgendwann nach Odessa und ist hier hängen geblieben. *„Odessa ist eine hervorragende Stadt in Bezug auf die künstlerischen Möglichkeiten und Traditionen."*

The 'Stoljarsky' School has a seventy-year history. Its founder was the Odessite violinist and music teacher Pjotr Solomonovitch Stoljarsky (1871–1944).

The school has trained many famous musicians: the pianist Boris Bloch and the violinist Michail Weiman as well as the world-famous David Oistrach.

Joint recitals by the young musicians from Odessa and Bern, which take place, for example, at the newly restored Odessa philharmonic hall, are the high points of the musical cooperation, as a result of which many friendships are formed between the children and youngsters.

Im Atelier des Malers Konstantin Silen
The studio of the painter Konstantin Silen

Der Besuch in seinem Atelier beginnt mit einem abenteuerlichen Gang über mehrere Hinterhöfe, vorbei an gefährlichen Gullydeckeln, fünf Stufen abwärts in einen düsteren Kellereingang. Hier bietet sich das Bild eines wahren Künstlerhaushaltes: Ein Chaos aus halbvollen Tee- und Rotweingläsern, eine misstrauische Katze, überfüllte Aschenbecher und eine geöffnete Fischdose nebst trockenem Brot – das ist der ca. sechs Quadratmeter große Vorraum zu einem etwas üppigerem ‚Atelier', welches sich türlos anschließt. Konstantin Silen arbeitet vielfältig, malt in Öl und Aquarell, Porträts oder abstrakt. Seine Bilder breitet er bereitwillig zur Begutachtung auf dem Boden aus. So wie er leben viele Künstler in Odessa. Doch nur wenigen von ihnen ist es vergönnt, ihre Werke in einer der größeren Galerien in Odessa auszustellen. Ihr Ruhm kommt später – vielleicht.

Eine Kunst muss noch erwähnt werden: Die des Schachspiels. Jede Stadt in der ehemaligen Sowjetunion hat einen Platz, meist in einem Park, an dem sich die Liebhaber des Brettspiels treffen. In Odessa findet man die meist älteren Strategen im Park gegenüber dem Hotel ‚Passage' am oberen Ende der Deribassowskaja. Hier warten sie vom frühen Morgen bis zum späten Abend auf ihre Gegner und analysieren die Partien der letzten Weltmeisterschaften.

"Real art is created in the cellar!" says talented painter Konstantin Silen confidently. He is not forced to offer his work for sale at the arts and crafts market in the city gardens, but is able to sell a few pictures through small exhibitions and is given commissions by the city or clients from the 'neighbouring' countries of Finland or Germany. He has worked in Görlitz, Stuttgart and Tübingen. Konstantin Silen graduated in architecture from Moscow University, came to Odessa and has somehow remained here. "Odessa is an excellent city where the possibilities for artists and artistic tradition is concerned."

A visitor wishing to view his studio has to find the way across a series of treacherous back yards, full of dangerous man-hole covers, down five steps to a dingy basement door. Behind the door lies a true bohemian household: a host of half-empty teacups and wineglasses, a suspicious cat, ashtrays full to the brim and an open tin of fish with a crust of stale bread fill the six square metres of ante-room which lead to the slightly larger 'studio', separated from the hall by a doorless frame only. Konstantin Silen's work varies widely, he uses oil and watercolour, his subjects range from portraits to the abstract. Many artists in Odessa live like he does. But only few see their work exhibited at one of the major art galleries in Odessa. Their fame will come later – perhaps.

One further art needs to be mentioned: the art of playing chess. Every town in the former Soviet Union has a place, usually a park, where players of the board game assemble. In Odessa the amateurs of the game, usually elderly gentlemen, meet in the park opposite the 'Passage' hotel at the top end of Deribasovskaya Street. Here, they wait from early morning to late evening for potential opponents, develop stratagems or sit analysing the latest world championship matches.

Warten auf den Gegner
Waiting for the opponent

Die neu erbaute Galerie im ‚Meeresbahnhof' zeigt Werke in- und ausländischer Künstler.
The newly erected gallery at the 'Morvoksal' shows works by local and international artists.

Schach: Die Kunst des Denkens hat in Odessa viele Freunde.
Chess: The art of thinking is very popular in Odessa.

Arkadia:
Sonne und Erholung
an den Stränden der Stadt

Arcadia:

sunny days on the city's beaches

88 Nach dem Zusammenbruch der Sowjetunion und der damit verbundenen wirtschaftlichen Neugestaltung sind sowohl die örtliche Verwaltung, als auch private Unternehmen bemüht, wieder verstärkt Besucher in die Stadt zu locken. Odessa ist seit jeher ein beliebter Ort für Erholungssuchende. Nicht nur, weil die Stadt als multikulturelles Zentrum eine große Attraktivität besitzt, insbesondere ist es auch das typische Klima, das die Menschen hierher zieht.

Odessa liegt zwischen dem 46. und 47. nördlichen Breitengrad und damit auf einer Höhe mit Szeged in Ungarn, Bern und La Rochelle. Ein vorwiegend gemäßigtes und trockenes Kontinentalklima bringt der Region, beeinflusst von der See, einen kurzen, milden Winter und einen heißen Sommer. Die Durchschnittstemperatur liegt bei 24°C, wobei Spitzenwerte von 40°C keine Seltenheit sind. Zum Glück sorgt eine angenehme Meeresbrise für frische und saubere Luft in der Stadt – daher ist Smog trotz zunehmender Verkehrsdichte die Ausnahme. Beliebt bei allen Einwohnern und Besuchern sind die etwas abseits vom Stadtzentrum gelegenen Badestrände.

Ausgangspunkt für einen ausgedehnten Spaziergang könnte das südliche Ende der Deribassowskaja sein. Hier steht seit wenigen Jahren ein Denkmal für den Türkenbezwinger José de Ribas. Linker Hand befindet sich das gewaltige Einfahrtstor zum Hafengelände, durch das man nur mit einem speziellen Ausweis gelangt. Schon von weitem ist das kreisende Spiel der Kräne zu beobachten – viele haben noch die Aufschrift ‚Takraf' und stammen aus ehemaliger DDR-Produktion.

Since the fall of communism and the beginning of the economic reforms both the city and private enterprises have been trying to revive the tourist trade in the city. Odessa has always been a popular resort for holidaymakers. It is not just the attraction of the colourful, multicultural city, but also and above all the typical climate which brings visitors to Odessa.

Odessa lies between latitudes 46 and 47, on a level with Szeged in Hungaria, Bern and La Rochelle. The climate is continental, dry but not extreme, is influenced by the sea and brings Odessa short, mild winters and hot summers. The average temperature is around 24°C and top temperatures of 40°C are quite common. Luckily, cool winds from the sea provide fresh, clean air for the city, so that smog conditions are the great exception in spite of the rising number of vehicles. The beaches situated a little way away from the city centre are popular with both the population of Odessa and guests to the city.

A good place to begin an extended walk along the coast is the south end of Deribasovskaya Street. A monument to the conqueror of the Turkish fortress, José de Ribas, was erected here a few years ago. On the left are the huge gates to the harbour area which only people equipped with a pass can enter. From far off, it is possible to see the cranes' circling motions – many of them still bear the inscription 'Takraf' and were produced in the former German Democratic Republic.

Ehrenmal zum Gedenken an die Befreiung der Stadt Odessa von deutschen und rumänischen Besatzungstruppen am 10. April 1944
Monument in commemoration of the liberation of Odessa from German and Rumanian occupation on 10 April 1944

Restaurants und Imbissstände an den Uferpromenaden:
Speisen und Getränke für den großen und den kleinen Geldbeutel
Restaurants and snack stalls by the coastal promenades:
food and drink whatever your budget

Arkadia ist bei den Einheimischen und den Touristen der beliebteste Strand in Odessa.
Arcadia is the most popular beach in Odessa, both among the locals and the tourists.

Nach zehn Minuten Fußweg kommt man zum größten Park der Stadt – dem ‚Schewtschenko'-Park. Hierher zieht es an Wochenenden die ‚Bolelschtschiki', die Fans des Fußballclubs ‚Tschernomorez Odessa'. Derzeit hat die Mannschaft im Kampf um die ukrainische Meisterschaft jedoch kaum ein Wörtchen mitzureden. Nicht weit vom Stadion – sozusagen mit Meeresblick – erhebt sich das Denkmal für den Unbekannten Matrosen. Zur Sowjetzeit standen hier von morgens bis abends kleine ‚Pioniere', die jeweils für eine Stunde symbolisch mit einem Holzgewehr Wache hielten – für die auserwählten Kinder eine Auszeichnung. Diese Tradition hat man abgeschafft, heute trifft man im Park eher Kinder mit einer Cola- oder Bierflasche in der Hand.

Bis zum Strand ‚Langeron' sind es nur wenige Minuten. Der helle feinkörnige Sandstrand bietet auf einer Breite von bis zu vierzig Metern Platz für alle Erholungssuchenden. An heißen Sommerwochenenden dagegen wird es sehr eng.

Die durchschnittliche Wassertemperatur liegt im Juli und August bei angenehmen 23°C. Die Strände von Odessa sind durch die Bucht geschützt, so dass es kaum zu hohen Wellen kommt. Da das Strandufer seicht ins Meer führt, ist auch für kleinere Kinder ein ungefährlicher Badespaß garantiert. Neuerdings bieten Aqua-Parks und andere Freizeiteinrichtungen vergnügliche Abwechslung, ein weiteres Zeichen des sich vollziehenden Wandels.

Nach einer Stunde gemütlichen Fußmarsches, vorbei an Strandpromenaden, Restaurants und Sanatorien, gelangt man zum beliebtesten Freizeit- und Erholungsgebiet von Odessa: Arkadia. Bereits ab Mitte des 19. Jahrhunderts, als die Stadtgrenze von Odessa noch in der Nähe der Deribassowskaja lag, ließen sich wohlhabende Bürger ihre ‚Datscha' in Arkadia bauen. Das Gebiet entwickelte sich schnell zu einem beliebten Ausflugsziel: Restaurants, Kur- und Erholungsheime schossen wie Pilze aus dem Boden. Die heilende Wirkung des salzhaltigen Schlammes aus den Mündungsgebieten der Flüsse ist weit über die Odessaer Grenzen hinaus bekannt. Heute liegt Arkadia längst innerhalb des Stadtgebietes.

A further ten minutes walk brings us to the city's biggest park, 'Shevtchenko' park. This is where, at the weekends, the 'bolelshtshiki', the fans of the football club 'Tchernomorets Odessa' assemble. At present, however, the team is far removed from any hopes of Ukrainian championship glory. Not far from the stadium stands the Monument to the Unknown Sailor, a monument with a view, so to speak. During the Soviet period, young 'pioneers' stood guard here from morning to night, for an hour each, armed with a symbolic wooden gun. For the children chosen this was considered a great honour. This tradition however has been abolished, nowadays you are more likely to find children hanging around the park with a bottle of coke or beer.

Only a couple of minutes further on lies 'Langeron' beach. The beach with its pale, fine sand is forty metres wide in places and in theory provides plenty of space for all who wish to bathe here. Nevertheless, on hot summer days, things can get a bit tight. In July and August the average temperature of the water is a pleasant 23°C. The beaches of Odessa are protected by the bay, so that large waves or surf are rare. As the beach slopes gently into the sea, even small children can play in the water without very much danger. A further sign of the changing times are Aqua Parks and other leisure facilities, which offer a welcome change from sea bathing.

Ausgefallene Konstruktionen für Restaurants ...
Unusual constructions for restaurants ...

In den letzten Jahren sind hier, am beliebtesten Strand von Odessa, wunderschöne Gebäudeanlagen mit Hotel- und Restaurantbetrieb entstanden. Traditionsgemäß besitzen sie meist ausländische Namen, wie z.B. das griechische ‚Ithaka'. Tagsüber wird man von sehr höflichem Personal verwöhnt, was vor zehn Jahren noch unvorstellbar war. Am Abend gibt es – jedenfalls in den warmen Sommermonaten – Musik, Disco, Tanz und Shows bis spät in die Nacht. Die Veränderungen sind offensichtlich und man fragt sich immer wieder: Woher kommt das viele Geld für die Investitionen?

Zurück ins Stadtzentrum gelangt man am besten mit einem Taxi. Die Fahrt dauert eine Viertelstunde und kostet ca. 20 Griwna, ungefähr vier Euro. Der Preis lässt sich verhandeln, doch nicht jeder Taxifahrer ist so ein Witzbold wie der aus folgender Anekdote:
Fahrer: „Na Jungs, wie viel habt Ihr nach der Nacht in Arkadia noch übrig?"
Gast (nachdenklich): „... so ungefähr dreizehn ..."
Fahrer: „Und, wohin soll es gehen?"
Gast: „Zur Deribassowskaja!"
Fahrer (überlegt): „... na los, haut Euch rein in meinen Mercedes, auch wenn ich durch Euch arm werde!"

After about an hour's unhurried walk along beach promenades, past restaurants and sanatoriums, the most popular holiday and leisure-district in Odessa comes into sight: Arcadia. From the mid-nineteenth century onwards, when the precincts of the city were still close to Deribasovskaya, wealthy citizens had their 'datshas' built in Arcadia. The area quickly became a popular destination for all kinds of excursions: Restaurants, sanatoriums and holiday accommodation shot up at lightning speed. The beneficial properties of the saline mud from the estuary of the rivers are famous far beyond the borders of Odessa. Today, Arcadia lies well within the confines of the city.

In the past few years, beautifully designed hotel and restaurant developments have been erected along this most popular beach in Odessa. Following a local tradition they usually have foreign names, such as the Greek 'Ithaka'. In the day time, polite, well trained staff cater to the guests' every wish, something completely unimaginable just over ten years ago. The evenings, during the summer months at least, are filled with a variety of entertainment – music, dancing, club nights and shows go on until the early hours of the morning. The changes are obvious and the question presents itself: Where does all the money that has been invested come from?

The best way to get back to the city centre is by taxi. It is about a quarter of an hour's drive and should cost about twenty grivna, approximately four euros. This price can be negotiated, but not all the taxi drivers are as good natured as the one in the following anecdote.
Driver: "Well lads, how much money have you got left after your night out in Arcadia?"
Client (trying to think): "... possibly thirteen ..."
Driver: "And where are you hoping to go?"
Client: "To Deribasovskaya!"
Driver (after a moment's consideration): "... ah, well, guys, pile into my Merc, and may I get poor tonight!"

**... bieten nachts eindrucksvolle Kulissen
für Varieté, Tanz und Disco.**
*... serve as great backdrops for variety shows,
dancing and clubbing at night.*

Kont. II
werden - würde - geworden
würde
haben - hätte - gehabt
wäre
sein - war - gewesen

„*Njemzi*":
Deutsche Spuren am Schwarzen Meer

'Njemzi':
a brief German history of Odessa

Neuburg bei Odessa: Valeri Zybakow leitet mehrere kleine Handwerksbetriebe.
Neuburg near Odessa: Valery Zybakov runs several small craftsmen's firms here.

Odessa is a comparatively young city. Little more than two hundred years ago, the Turkish stronghold Khadzhi-Bej was turned into a Russian settlement from which the city of Odessa then developed. Ever since the founding days, Germans (in Russian: njemzi) have lived here by the Black Sea.

The areas in the south of the Russian empire were very sparsely populated. At the beginning of the nineteenth century, many Russians were still serfs and this was a barrier to rapid settlement in the region. Both Catherine II and Alexander I made great efforts to attract settlers from all over Europe, but especially from the German states, to the area by offering political and economic privileges. According to the records, the first farmers from Baden, Württemberg and Bavaria arrived in the Black Sea region in 1803 by way of the Danube. Theirs was a journey into the uncertain, accompanied by hardship, hunger, illness and death. The construction of German settlements in the area around Odessa progressed rapidly throughout the early years of the nineteenth century. New methods in crop growing and cattle farming made the settlers modestly wealthy.

German craftsmen and merchants soon settled within the city itself. The 'Passage' belonged to the plant dealer Julius Rothe. The owner of the largest department store on the corner of Deribasovskaya and Ekaterin Street was the merchant Wilhelm Wagner. One of the most influential families in Odessa in the tsars' day was the Falz-Fein family, who made a fortune in the animal and grain trade. Their mansion in Gogol Street with its huge sculptures has become one of the symbols of the city. Friedrich Falz-Fein, the last member of the family to live in Odessa, founded the well-known 'Askania Nova' Nature Park. When the communists grabbed power in Odessa in 1920, the family managed to escape aboard the last émigréship.

Odessa ist eine relativ junge Stadt. Vor etwas mehr als 200 Jahren wurde aus der ehemals türkischen Festung Hadshibej die russische Ansiedlung und später die Stadt Odessa. Seit dieser Zeit lebten und leben auch Deutsche (russisch: ‚njemzi') hier am Schwarzen Meer.

Die Gebiete im Süden des zaristischen Russland waren nur sehr gering bevölkert. Die Anfang des 19. Jahrhunderts noch existierende Leibeigenschaft war ein Hemmnis bei der schnellen Besiedlung der Regionen. Sowohl Katharina II., als auch Zar Alexander I. unternahmen diverse Anstrengungen, Menschen aus ganz unterschiedlichen Teilen Europas, insbesondere aber aus den deutschen Staaten, mittels politischer und ökonomischer Vergünstigungen ins Land zu locken.

Die ersten Bauern aus Baden, Württemberg und Bayern erreichten nachweislich im Jahre 1803 über die Donau das Schwarzmeergebiet. Es war eine Reise ins Ungewisse, begleitet von Strapazen, Hunger, Krankheit und Tod. Der Ausbau deutscher Siedlungen in Gebieten um Odessa Anfang des 19. Jahrhunderts ging zügig voran. Neue Methoden in Ackerbau und Viehzucht verhalfen den Kolonisten zu bescheidenem Wohlstand.

Großliebenthal was the German colony closest to Odessa. It consisted of several villages which were situated along the so-called 'German canyon'. An hour's drive away is Neuburg (Novogradovka). Here, with the help of the Gesellschaft für Technische Zusammenarbeit (GTZ), an agency for international cooperation owned by the German government, a business park and new homes have been built for the descendants of Germans deported by Stalin. Many of them came here from Kazakhstan, with very little to call their own. One of them is Valery Zybakov, whose unsettled family history is typical of so many others, "My mother and my grandmother were Germans, they were born here in Neuburg. During the war they were all deported to Poland, from Poland to Germany, from there to the Soviet Union, to Kazakhstan. They suffered what many Germans from the Soviet Union did. After the treaty between Chancellor Kohl and the Ukrainian President Leonid Kravchuk in 1992 we came back here, to the land of our forefathers." Valery Zybakov is now director of a small-scale business park consisting of several craftsmens' firms. He has achieved this by a combination of hard work and financial support from Germany.

The Lutheran congregation in Odessa can also look back on a two hundred year history. For the first few years, the community was run on a shoestring, but in 1827 St Paul's Church was inaugurated. The architect was none less than Franz Boffo, mastermind of the 'Potemkin' highlights around Odessa.

In der Stadt selbst ließen sich alsbald deutsche Handwerker und Kaufleute nieder. Die ‚Passage' gehörte dem Pflanzenhändler Julius Rothe, der Besitzer des größten Warenhauses an der Ecke Deribassowskaja/Ekatarinenstraße war der Kaufmann Wilhelm Wagner. Eine der einflussreichsten Familien im zaristischen Odessa war die Familie Falz-Fein, die durch Viehzucht und Getreidehandel zu großem Reichtum gelangte. Ihr Wohnhaus in der Gogolstraße mit den gewaltigen Atlanten gehört heute zu den Wahrzeichen der Stadt. Friedrich Falz-Fein, letzter Vertreter der Familie in Odessa, gründete den berühmten Naturpark ‚Askania Nowa'. Als die Kommunisten im Jahre 1920 auch in Odessa die Macht an sich rissen, flüchtete die Familie mit dem letzten Emigrantenschiff ins Ausland.

Großliebenthal war die der Stadt Odessa am nächsten gelegene deutsche Kolonie. Zu ihr gehörten mehrere Dörfer, die entlang der sogenannten ‚Deutschen Schlucht' liegen. Mit dem Auto ist man in einer Stunde in Neuburg (Nowogradowka) Hier entstanden mit Unterstützung der Gesellschaft für Technische Zusammenarbeit (GTZ) ein Gewerbepark und Wohnhäuser, in denen die Nachkommen der durch Stalin deportierten Deutschen wieder ein neues Zuhause fanden. Die meisten von ihnen kamen mit wenig Hab und Gut aus Kasachstan. Einer von ihnen ist Valeri Zybakow, dessen bewegte Familiengeschichte stellvertretend für viele andere steht.

Die St. Pauls-Kirche fiel im Jahre 1976 einem Brand zum Opfer. Neben der Ruine wurde im September 2002 das Pastorenhaus eingeweiht.

St Paul's church was destroyed by a fire in 1976. In 2002 the pastor's house was inaugurated next to the ruin.

Over time, the church became too small for the growing congregation and needed repairs. In 1897, a new church was erected in its place, large enough to accommodate the members of the congregation, more than seven thousand in all. Stalin's policies brought an end to the life of the Lutheran community. Most of the 350,000 Germans living in Ukraine disappeared – they were dispossessed, had to flee, were deported or shot outright.

The building of St Paul's church was destroyed in 1976, when a fire was laid there. Only after Perestroika was a revival of Lutheran life in Odessa possible. In 1990 the German congregation was reassembled and just a few years later the church building once again became the property of the parish.

„Meine Mutter und meine Großmutter waren Deutsche, sie wurden hier in Neuburg geboren. Im Krieg wurden alle nach Polen deportiert, von Polen nach Deutschland, von da in die Sowjetunion, nach Kasachstan. Sie sind den Leidensweg gegangen, den viele Deutsche aus der Sowjetunion gehen mussten. Nach dem Abkommen zwischen Kanzler Kohl und dem ukrainischen Präsidenten Leonid Kravtschuk von 1992 sind wir dann hierher zurückgekehrt, auf den Boden unserer Vorfahren." Heute ist Valeri Zybakow Chef in einem Gewerbepark mit mehreren kleinen Handwerksbetrieben. Aufgebaut hat er das mit viel Schweiß sowie mit materieller und finanzieller Unterstützung aus Deutschland.

Next to the church is the pastor's house, which was inaugurated during a festive service on September 23rd, 2002, following lengthy and expensive restoration work. After many years of enforced absence, the German Lutheran church has now regained a home in Odessa, complete with a deaconry, rooms for a soup kitchen and a few seminar and guestrooms.

The future fate of St Paul's church itself on the other hand is uncertain. Containing seating for a thousand two hundred parishioners, it was the largest and most important neo-Romanesque building in the Ukraine. The cost of rebuilding it is estimated at several million euros, a sum far too large for the tiny congregation, consisting of five hundred members only, to raise. Compromise solutions are therefore being considered: One option is to restore only the back section of the church and to preserve the rest as a ruin.

Auch die evangelisch-lutherische Kirche in Odessa kann auf eine 200-jährige Geschichte zurückblicken. In den ersten Jahren arbeitete die Gemeinde unter extrem bescheidenen Verhältnissen, doch schon 1827 wurde die St. Pauls-Kirche eingeweiht. Der Architekt war kein geringerer als Franz Boffo, Konstrukteur der ‚Potemkin'-Treppe und anderer architektonischer Perlen in Odessa.

Mit den Jahren wurde das Kirchengebäude baufällig und für die wachsende Gemeinde zu klein. An seiner Stelle wurde im Jahre 1897 eine neue Kirche errichtet, die den über 7000 Mitgliedern ausreichend Platz bot. Das Schicksal der deutschen Gemeinde wurde durch die Stalinpolitik besiegelt. Die meisten der 350.000 in der Ukraine lebenden Deutschen verschwanden – enteignet, geflüchtet, deportiert oder erschossen.

Das Gebäude der St. Pauls-Kirche fiel 1976 einer Brandstiftung zum Opfer. Einen Neuanfang des evangelischen Kirchenlebens gab es in Odessa erst nach der Perestroika. 1990 fand sich die deutsche Gemeinde zusammen, wenige Jahre später konnte sie das Gotteshaus wieder ihr Eigentum nennen.

Neben der Kirche befindet sich das Pastorenhaus, das nach umfangreicher und teurer Rekonstruktion am 23. September 2002 feierlich mit einem Gottesdienst eingeweiht wurde. Somit hat die deutsche evangelisch-lutherische Gemeinde in Odessa nach vielen Jahren wieder eine Heimstatt mit angeschlossener Diakonie, Räumlichkeiten für die Armenspeisung sowie einige Ausbildungs- und Gästezimmer.

Das künftige Schicksal der St. Pauls-Kirche liegt allerdings in „Gottes Hand". Mit 1200 Sitzplätzen war sie das größte und historisch wertvollste neuromanische Bauwerk in der Ukraine. Ein Wiederaufbau wird auf mehrere Millionen Euro geschätzt, zuviel für die kleine Gemeinde, die heute rund 500 Mitglieder zählt. Daher wird nach Kompromissen gesucht: So überlegt man, nur einen Teil der Kirche zu restaurieren und den Rest als Ruine zu belassen.

For around four hundred German prisoners of war Odessa became the final resting place. A cemetery on the edge of town, built in 1999, recalls their fate. The Volksbund Deutsche Kriegsgräberfürsorge e.V., the German war graves association, commissioned the graveyard. The German building contractor Paul Louis who runs a business in Odessa took on the construction work. Lawn areas, grave stones and a memorial tablet were erected, along with living quarters for the caretaker in charge of looking after and guarding the cemetery. Differences in opinion between the contractor and the war graves association meant that, for a while, the cemetery was somewhat run down, but these differences seem to have been resolved now.

Many young Germans used to pass St Paul's Church every day in the 70's and 80's of the past century, without giving it particular attention. These youngsters were students from the former German Democratic Republic on the way from their student halls along Komsomolskaya Street to the main building of the university. The life of the future physicists, chemists and mathematicians took place between the lecture theatre and their student accommodation. Four students shared approximately twenty square meters. During leisure periods sport was popular, particularly table tennis, volleyball or football, but only if the time was not taken up with the daily foray for food supplies. Visits to the lovely opera house were rare and interesting films at the cinema the exception. In the summer season, the students lay on the beach at Arcadia, trying to swot up for their exams and everyone was glad to be able to go home in the break between semesters. Several hundred young Germans graduated from the University of Odessa, the Polytechnic Institute or the Institute of Economy. Quite a few brought Russian wives back to the German Democratic Republic.

Hunderte deutscher Kriegsgefangener fanden auf einem Odessaer Friedhof ihre letzte Ruhe. *Hundreds of German POW's are buried in an Odessa cemetery.*

Die Staatliche ‚Metschnikow'-Universität ist die bedeutendste Bildungseinrichtung.
The 'Metchnikov' State University is the most important educational institution.

Für ungefähr 400 Kriegsgefangene war Odessa die letzte Station ihres Lebens. Seit 1999 erinnert ein Friedhof am Stadtrand an ihr Schicksal. Der Volksbund Deutsche Kriegsgräberfürsorge e.V. gab dafür den Auftrag. Der in Odessa ansässige deutsche Bauunternehmer Paul Louis führte die Arbeiten durch. Eine Anlage mit Grünflächen, Grabsteinen und Gedenktafel entstand, darauf ein kleines Wohnhaus für das Personal, das für Pflege und Bewachung zuständig ist. Unstimmigkeiten zwischen dem Volksbund und dem Bauunternehmer ließen den Friedhof teilweise verwahrlosen, sind nun aber größtenteils behoben.

Fast täglich gingen viele junge Deutsche in den 70-er und 80-er Jahren des vorigen Jahrhunderts an der St. Pauls-Kirche vorbei, ohne jedoch allzu große Notiz von ihr zu nehmen. Es waren DDR-Studenten auf dem Weg von ihrem Wohnheim in der Komsomolskaja-Straße zum Hauptgebäude der Universität. Das Leben der angehenden Physiker, Chemiker und Mathematiker spielte sich fünf Jahre lang zwischen Vorlesungssaal und Studentenbude ab. Vier Personen mussten sich knapp zwanzig Quadratmeter teilen. In der Freizeit war Sport – bevorzugt Tischtennis, Fußball und Volleyball – beliebt, allerdings nur, wenn die täglichen ‚Nahrungsmittelbeschaffungsmaßnahmen' es zeitlich erlaubten. Besuche des wunderschönen Operntheaters waren selten und interessante Kinofilme die Ausnahme. In der Sommersaison bereiteten sich die Studenten am Strand von Arkadia auf die Prüfung vor und alle waren heilfroh, in den Semesterferien nach Hause fahren zu können. Mehrere hundert junge Deutsche beendeten in Odessa ihr Studium, an der Universität, dem Polytechnischen Institut oder dem Institut für Volkswirtschaft. So mancher kehrte mit einer russischen Ehefrau in die DDR zurück.

Heute sind Studenten aus Deutschland wieder des öfteren in der Stadt anzutreffen. Sie verbringen hier einige Tage oder Wochen und kommen meistens aus Regensburg, denn die dortige Universität pflegt die Kontakte zur hiesigen Partner-Universität seit über zehn Jahren.

Nowadays, German students are again becoming more frequent visitors to Odessa. They spend a few days or weeks in the city and usually come from Regensburg. The university there has been keeping up links with its Ukrainian partner university for more than ten years.

The 'Bayerisches Haus Odessa' is a meeting place in Odessa for Germans and others interested in German culture, research and economics. The house which is supported financially by the German federal states of Bavaria and Saxony, the Gesellschaft für Technische Zusammenarbeit, the Bavarian Lutheran church and other institutions, organises many events providing information to those interested. There are also language courses on the schedule. A well-stocked library and reading room has been provided through cooperation with the Goethe Institute and there is also a kindergarten operated by the 'Bayerisches Haus'. Of particular importance is the concert and music department which runs a choir and orchestra. Within the 'Bayerisches Haus' there is also a centre for management training, which provides seminars on management skills to Ukrainian entrepreneurs.

'Consulting Odessa' says the business card of Jürgen Mewis, who started his business in Odessa in 1995. Immediately after the fall of communism he realised that the states of the former Soviet Union might be the place to start a new enterprise. Having graduated from Moscow University in engineering science with a specialisation in the area of constructing nuclear power plants, he saw little future after 1989 in continuing in his profession. He moved to Kiev first, where he founded a joint venture offering business consulting services, then relocated to Odessa. He says that coming to Odessa to him meant losing nothing and gaining almost everything. To be successful it is necessary, according to him, to know the way of thinking and the local customs, the language, and to have the

Ein Zentrum für Deutsche in Odessa, aber auch für alle, die sich für deutsche Kultur, Wissenschaft und Wirtschaft interessieren, ist das ‚Bayerische Haus Odessa'. Gefördert u.a. von den Ländern Bayern und Sachsen, der Gesellschaft für Technische Zusammenarbeit und der evangelisch-lutherischen Kirche in Bayern bietet das ‚Bayerische Haus' den Interessenten zahlreiche Informationsveranstaltungen an. Außerdem besteht die Möglichkeit zur Teilnahme an Sprachkursen. In Kooperation mit dem Goethe-Institut steht eine umfangreiche Bibliothek mit Lesesaal zur Verfügung, wobei das ‚Bayerische Haus' auch einen Kindergarten unterhält. Von ganz besonderer Bedeutung ist die Konzert- und Musikabteilung mit Chor und Orchester. Innerhalb des ‚Bayerischen Hauses' arbeitet ein Management-Trainingszentrum. Hier können sich ukrainische Unternehmer in speziellen Seminaren weiterbilden.

‚Consulting Odessa' steht auf der Visitenkarte von Jürgen Mewis, der seit 1995 in Odessa als Unternehmer arbeitet. Gleich nach der Wende in Deutschland hat er die Chance erkannt, in den Ländern der ehemaligen Sowjetunion etwas Neues auf die Beine stellen zu können. Jürgen Mewis studierte in Moskau Atomkraftwerksanlagenbau und sah nach 1989 kaum Chancen in seinem Beruf. Er ging erst nach Kiew, wo er ein Joint Venture für Unternehmensberatung gründete und kam dann nach Odessa. Er habe hier nichts verloren, sondern fast alles gefunden, meint er. Was man brauche, um erfolgreich zu sein, sei die Kenntnis der Mentalität und der Gepflogenheiten, das Beherrschen der Sprache und die Fähigkeit, mit Leuten vor Ort Projekte zu realisieren. Über die Stadt selbst sagt Jürgen Mewis: *„Odessa hatte für mich schon als Student immer einen anziehenden Klang, ich mag die Stadt, auch wenn sie in vielen Punkten noch Nachholbedarf hat. Die Architektur ist an den meisten Stellen heruntergekommen, die Strand- und Uferzonen müssen unbedingt erneuert werden, …. aber alles in allem: ich mag diese Stadt mit ihren beeindruckenden Bauwerken und den hübschen Frauen. Ich bin mit einer Odessitin verheiratet."*

capacity to put into practice projects with people on the spot. On the topic of the city itself, Jürgen Mewis adds, "The name Odessa has always had an attractive sound to it, ever since I was a student. I like the city, even if in many ways it has a long way to go. The architecture is run down in many places, the beaches and coastline urgently need a facelift, … but, on the whole, I like the city with its magnificent buildings and pretty women. I am married to a girl from Odessa."

There are many reasons for coming to Odessa and many reasons to stay a long time. In 2000, the Deutsche Industrie und Handelskammer (DIHK), the German Chamber of Trade and Industry opened an office in Odessa, just round the corner from the GTZ, in a first class location, hardly more than hundred metres from the 'Potemkin' Stairway.

There, Rainer Kiewel looks after German entrepreneurs hoping to set up business ventures in the region. He also knows the Ukrainian customs and way of life well: After studying in Lwow (Lemberg) he worked as a radar engineer in Löbau in Germany – his first life, as he likes to put it. For the last ten years he has lived in Odessa.

Es gibt viele Gründe, nach Odessa zu kommen und für lange Zeit zu bleiben. Seit dem Jahr 2000 hat die Deutsche Industrie- und Handelskammer (DIHK) ein Büro, gleich in der Nachbarschaft zur GTZ, in hervorragender Lage, nur etwas mehr als hundert Meter zur ‚Potemkin'-Treppe. Rainer Kiewel ist Ansprechpartner für deutsche Unternehmer, die in der Region Geschäfte machen möchten. Auch er kennt die Gepflogenheiten von Land und Leuten gut: Nach dem Studium in Lwow (Lemberg) war er Radartechniker in Löbau – in seinem ersten Leben, wie er sagt. Seit zehn Jahren ist er nun in Odessa. Hier gründete Rainer Kiewel einen Optikerladen mit speziell geschliffenen Brillengläsern und einem großen Sortiment an Gestellen. „Eine feine Sache damals", sagt er. „Es gab schon genug ‚Neureiche' und man konnte Geld abschöpfen, unwahrscheinlich."

In das DIHK-Büro kommen deutsche Unternehmer, die in Odessa Geschäfte machen oder vermitteln wollen: Dazu zählen Bauunternehmer, Experten für Recycling und Containerlogistik. Sie alle erhalten Unterstützung in organisatorischen und rechtlichen Fragen. Die Bedingungen vor Ort sind nicht die schlechtesten. Die Hafenstadt hatte schon in Sowjetzeiten eine gut funktionierende Infrastruktur, die Transportwege waren ausgebaut und der Hafen ist auch im Winter eisfrei.

Die größten Hürden für deutsche Unternehmer stecken meistens im Detail, oben an stehen Bürokratie und Korruption. Weil in Odessa Arbeitnehmer wenig verdienen, ist die Verlockung groß, überall die Hand aufzuhalten. Doch Rainer Kiewel warnt vor Schmiergeldzahlungen. „Man kommt da in einen Teufelskreis. Wer hier vor Ort nicht versteht, mit dem Beziehungsgeflecht, das für Geschäfte erforderlich ist, zurechtzukommen, der macht keine Geschäfte."

Rainer Kiewel hat sich in Odessa eingelebt. Auch er hat hier sein privates Glück – eine Odessitin – gefunden. Vielleicht, so meint er, werde er sogar sesshaft: „Odessa ist eine Superstadt, zu schade um zu Hause rumzusitzen."

Here, he opened an optician's shop selling made to measure lenses and a large variety of different frames. "At the time, this was a great business idea," he says. "Even then, there were plenty of 'nouveaux-riches' people around who were prepared to spend an incredible amount of money."

The DIHK office caters for German business men who plan to sign or negotiate contracts in Odessa: There are building contractors, experts for recycling or container logistics. They are all given advice on legal and practical matters. The preconditions for trade are not at all bad. The infrastructure of the city with its port worked smoothly even in Soviet days, the transportation routes were built to a high standard and the port never freezes up, even in winter.

The biggest obstacles for German businesses usually appear when sorting out the details of transactions, with bureaucracy and corruption being top of the list of potential headaches. Since the salaries and wages paid locally are very meagre, the temptation to make a little on the side is great. But Rainer Kiewel warns against giving bribes, "It's a vicious circle. People who don't understand and can't deal with the network of contacts necessary to do business here are not going to make any money."

Rainer Kiewel has got accustomed to Odessa. He also has found private happiness here – by marrying an Odessite. Perhaps, he says, he will settle here. "Odessa is a great city, a shame to sit around at home."

Sprachkurse im ‚Bayerischen Haus Odessa' sind meistens ausgebucht. *Language courses at the 'Bayerisches Haus Odessa' are usually booked out.*

„Businessmeni':
Arm wie du und reich wie ich

'Businessmeni':
getting rich, Odessa-style

Der Hafen – das war und ist das Tor zur Welt. Durch ihn entstanden der Mythos der Stadt, die zahlreichen Nationalitäten, die kulturelle Vielfalt, die Sehnsucht, die Hoffnung und das Warten, die schwerreichen Jungs und die armen leichten Mädchen.

Sah man früher an jeder Ecke Matrosen in ihren weiß-blauen Uniformen, so muss man sie heute eher suchen. Die ukrainische Flotte hat nach der Perestroika kräftig Federn gelassen. Schiffe wurden zum Vorteil einiger Weniger zu Spottpreisen in das Ausland verhökert. Viel seltener als früher legen Luxusliner im Hafen an, um dann eine Schar von Touristen in die Stadt zu spülen.

Der Warenumschlag hat zehn Jahre nach der politischen Wende noch nicht wieder das ehemalige Volumen erreicht. Dennoch, die Kräne im Hafen drehen sich.

Aber es soll nach Jahren des Verfalls wieder besser werden. Svetlana Kobyljanskaja von der Geschäftsleitung der Hafenholding ist voller Optimismus: *„Es gab mal so etwas wie eine Schwarzmeerflotte in der Ukraine, die aus insgesamt 334 großen Schiffen bestand. Dann ist alles zusammengebrochen, mit jedem neuen Präsidenten war es so, dass Schiffe immer irgendwann irgendwo an einem anderen Ort auftauchten und letztlich heute nur noch eines übrig ist. Der neue Transportminister kam nach seinem Amtsantritt gleich nach Odessa und sagte, dass alles getan werden müsse, um eine neue ukrainische Flotte aufzubauen."*

The port has always been and still is the gateway to the world. Odessa's reputation is founded on the port, the many nationalities, the many different cultures, the longing, hope and waiting, the big boys with the fat wallets and the poor girls walking the streets.

Sailors in their blue and white uniforms used to be a constant feature of Odessa, but have become quite rare now. The Ukrainian fleet was substantially reduced after Perestroika. Ships were sold off at bargain-basement prices to foreign buyers, with only a small number reaping the benefits. Luxury cruise liners, which used to regularly tie up in the port and release droves of tourists into the town, have become comparatively rare.

The volume of merchandise processed through the port ten years after the political change-over has not yet reached the levels of the past. Nevertheless, the cranes in the port are hard at work.

After years of decline things are now expected to get better. Svetlana Kobyljanskaya, a member of the board of directors of the holding company running the port is optimistic, "There used to be a sort of Black Sea fleet in the Ukraine, consisting of 334 big ships altogether. Then everything collapsed, with each new president of state more ships disappeared, only to pop up again in places where they didn't belong, now there is only one ship left. The new minister of transport visited Odessa immediately after coming into office and emphasised that everything has to be done to get a new Ukrainian fleet together."

In the meantime, modern technology is taking over the work in the port. A new centre for container logistics, for example, has been built with help and advice from Hamburg. Unfortunately, curious visitors are not usually admitted to the port area. With the help of a few tricks, dollars and contacts it is however possible to gain access.

Der Hafen ist seit jeher wirtschaftlicher Dreh- und Angelpunkt. Im Containerbereich entsteht ein Logistikzentrum mit Know How aus Hamburg.
The port has always been the economic hub. In the container section a new logistics centre is being built with know how from Hamburg.

Im ehemaligen Schahpalast befindet sich die Hauptgeschäftsstelle der ‚Schifffahrtsbank'.
The former Shah's palace now houses the headquarters of the 'Maritime Transport Bank'.

Mittlerweile übernimmt moderne Technik das Ruder im Hafen. So entstand z.B. ein neues Logistikzentrum für den Containerumschlag mit Know How aus Hamburg. Leider ist der Zutritt zum Hafengelände für neugierige Besucher gesperrt. Mit einigen Tricks, Dollars und Beziehungen schafft man es aber doch irgendwie.

Etwas einfacher ist es, in das Herz des Odessaer Finanzimperiums zu gelangen. Die ‚Schifffahrtsbank' ist eine der renommiertesten Geldinstitute der Ukraine. Hauptaktionäre sind Firmen in Großbritannien, der Schweiz und in den USA, aber auch bedeutende einheimische Unternehmen wie die Hafenholding oder der Ölgigant ‚Lukoil'. Die großen Kunden haben, nomen est omen, mit dem Hafen zu tun. Dazu kommen Firmen aus der Leichtindustrie und dem Ölgeschäft. Schließt man vom optischen Eindruck des Unternehmens auf seine finanzielle Situation, dann steht hier alles zum Besten. Jeder Passant kann sich von der Attraktivität des Gebäudes, es ist der Schahpalast in der Gogolstraße, überzeugen. Innen bietet der Einsatz moderner Computertechnik beste Geschäftsbedingungen, die Schließfächer im Keller sind nur unter strengsten Sicherheitsregeln erreichbar. Anonymität wird garantiert. Die ist auch notwendig, denn die Beträge, um die es hier geht, liegen häufig im Millionenbereich – in Dollar, versteht sich.

Getting to the heart of the Odessa financial empire is a little easier. The 'Maritime Transport Bank' is one of the best known financial institutions in the Ukraine. The main shareholders are firms in Great Britain, Switzerland and the US, but also major local firms such as the holding company for the port and the gigantic oil company 'Lukoil'. As the name 'Maritime Transport Bank' suggests, the largest clients are in the shipping business, but firms in the light industry and oil companies also bank here. If the appearance of the business premises is anything to go by, business is going well for the bank. From the outside, passers-by can take in the attractive exterior of the bank's building, the former Shah's palace in Gogol Street. On the inside, modern computer technology makes banking easy, while access to the safes in the cellar is only granted under the strictest security provisions. Anonymity is guaranteed. This is necessary, as the sums in question are substantial, often in the region of several million – dollars, of course.

"Business could be even better if Odessa was made a free trade zone" says Konstantin G. Goy, who has recently been made director of the bank and who used to be in charge of financial policy on the city council. The free trading zone however is a dream which the heads of the local economy have been nurturing for several years, but which has little chance of materialising. According to Konstantin Goy, the tourist trade also needs

Der ‚Privoz' ist der älteste Handelsplatz
von Odessa.
*The 'Privoz' market is the oldest trading place
in Odessa.*

„Es könnte noch besser laufen, wenn Odessa zur
Freihandelszone erklärt würde", meint der ‚frisch
gebackene' Bankdirektor Konstantin G. Goy, der zuvor
Finanzpolitiker im Stadtrat war. Doch die Freihandelszone ist ein Wunschtraum, der schon seit mehreren
Jahren in den Köpfen der Wirtschaftsbosse herum-
schwirrt. Auch der Tourismus müsse angekurbelt werden, denn Odessa habe etwas zum Vorzeigen und
überhaupt sei in Odessa eigentlich alles in Ordnung,
ist Konstantin Goy überzeugt. Die Gesetze seien gut,
sie müssten nur in die Praxis umgesetzt werden. Hier
paart sich Managerdenken mit Politikeroptimismus.

Wo, außer im Hafen, pulsiert das Leben am stärksten?
Auf dem ‚Privoz'. Das ist der Bauernmarkt oder Basar,
ganz in der Nähe des Hauptbahnhofes. Und wer nicht
glaubt, dass in Odessa Menschen aus über hundert
Nationalitäten leben, braucht nur eine Stunde über
den ‚Privoz' zu gehen. Es herrscht ein einziges
Geschiebe und Gerufe, Feilschen und Anpreisen:
Sonnenblumenöl aus Neuburg, Gewürze, Obst und
Gemüse aus dem Kaukasus oder Moldawien, Waren
aus der Türkei oder Rumänien.

*boosting, as Odessa has plenty to offer and, anyway,
there is nothing wrong with Odessa, he is quick to
assert. The laws, he says, are good, they only need to
be put into practice. At this point managerial calculation
meets political optimism.*

*Where else, apart from the port, is there plenty of life?
The place to go is called 'Privoz'. This is the bazaar or
farmers market close to the main railway station.
Anyone who does not believe that there are one hundred nationalities living in Odessa need only spend an
hour walking around the 'Privoz'. The market is full to
the brim with humanity, noisy bargaining and barte-
ring, traders plying their wares: sunflower oil from
Neuburg, spices, fruit and vegetables from the
Caucasus or Moldova, goods from Turkey or Rumania.*

Großhandelsmarkt ‚Siebter Kilometer‘: Tägliche Warenumsätze in Millionenhöhe sind garantiert.
The 'Seventh Kilometre' wholesale market: A daily turnover to the tune of several million dollars is guaranteed.

Der ‚Privoz‘ hat eine lange Tradition. Schon zu Beginn des 19. Jahrhunderts wurden auf einem großen freien Platz am Rande des Stadtkerns die Waren direkt vom Pferdewagen herunter verkauft. Mit steigender Einwohnerzahl nahm auch die Bedeutung des Marktes zu. Nach und nach entstanden die ersten Holzbaracken und dann kleinere Häuser. Die architektonisch wertvolle ‚Fruchtpassage‘, die 1913 gebaut wurde, ist heute noch Anziehungspunkt für viele Besucher. Ein neues Büchlein über Odessa sagt, dass *„die ‚Fruchtpassage‘ nicht schlecht erhalten ist"*, was bedeutet, dass das Gebäude einer dringenden Renovierung bedarf.

Ist der Besuch des ‚Privoz‘ für den Touristen durchaus interessant und unterhaltsam, so gibt es für den Abenteuerlustigen noch eine Steigerung: Der ‚Siebte Kilometer‘ – kurz ‚7. km‘ . Dahinter verbirgt sich eine einzigartige Odessaer Geschichte. Der Vorgänger des ‚7. km‘ hieß ‚Toltschock‘ – von den Odessiten liebevoll ‚Tultsche‘ genannt. Er war der berühmteste Schwarzmarkt in der gesamten Sowjetunion. Auch wenn die staatlichen Läden in der Stadt gähnend leer standen, gab es auf dem ‚Tultsche‘ buchstäblich alles: Scherzhaft übertrieben – also auf die typische Odessaer Art – konnte man hier vom rostigen Nagel bis zur Atombombe alles ‚organisieren‘. Vieles kam über den Hafen ins Land. Die Bedeutung dieses ‚Umschlagplatzes für heiße Waren‘ hat sich nach der Wende geändert.

The 'Privoz' has a long tradition. From the beginning of the nineteenth century onwards goods were sold directly off the back of horse drawn wagons in the open space just outside the town centre. With the rise in population, the market's importance grew. Bit by bit, early wooden shacks and small houses were erected. The 'fruit hall', which is of architectural interest, was erected in 1913 and still draws many visitors. A recent booklet on Odessa states that "the 'fruit hall' is in reasonable condition", meaning it is in urgent need of construction work.

A visit to the 'Privoz' may be interesting and entertaining for tourists, but the more adventurous may like to go a step further: to the 'Seventh Kilometre', '7th km' for short. This name stands for a unique Odessa story. The predecessor of the '7th km' was called 'Toltshok', known lovingly to the Odessites as 'Tultshe'. This was the most famous black market in the entire Soviet Union. Even when the state-owned shops in the centre were totally empty, more or less everything was available at the 'Tultshe': to put it in a slightly exaggerated way – that is to say in the typical Odessite way – it was possible to obtain everything here from a rusty nail to the atomic bomb. Lots of the wares arrived through the port. The importance of this 'trading place for goods of doubtful origin' has altered since the fall of communism.

Markt-Mobilität
Market mobility

Das Knabbern von Sonnenblumenkernen ist beliebt. Doch mit ihrem Verkauf wird man kaum reich. *Snacking on sunflower seeds is popular. But selling them is not going to make anyone rich fast.*

Multitalentierter Handwerker:
Einsetzen von Reißverschlüssen, Reparatur von
Elektrogeräten, Scheren schleifen, …
A craftsman of many talents: insertion of zips,
repair of electrical goods, sharpening of scissors …

Heute ist der ‚7. km' – er liegt am Kilometerstein ‚Sieben' einer großen Fernverkehrsstraße – der bedeutendste Großhandelsmarkt in der Ukraine. Er ist eine Stadt in der Stadt, ein Markt mit einem eigenen Straßennetz, Geschäften und einer kleinen Poliklinik. Die Warenlager befinden sich in aufeinandergestapelten Metall-Containern. Open-Air-Konzerte von Rockgruppen aus Russland sind an sommerlichen Abenden keine Seltenheit. Täglich bringen rund 500 Lastkraftwagen und Busse Händler aus der ganzen Ukraine hierher, die sich mit Waren eindecken, die vorher billig und in großen Mengen eingekauft wurden. Darunter viele Waren aus der Türkei, die irgendwie an den Zollbehörden vorbeigeschleust werden. Der ‚7. km' bietet einigen tausend Menschen in Odessa und Umgebung einen Arbeitsplatz, was bei der hohen Arbeitslosigkeit und dem niedrigen Lohnniveau ein nicht zu unterschätzender wirtschaftlicher Aspekt ist. Die Stadt erzielt dadurch gewaltige finanzielle Einnahmen und wie Kenner der Szene wissen, ist der ‚7. km' eine zusätzliche Geldquelle für manchen Staatsdiener. „Hier halten alle die Hand auf: Zoll, Miliz und wer weiß schon genau, wer hier auf welche Weise was verdient."

Auf dem Rückweg in die Stadt führt die Fahrt durch die Moldawanka, das berühmte Stadtviertel des Schriftstellers Isaak Babel. In der Moldawanka siedelten sich schon zu Beginn des 19. Jahrhunderts aus Moldawien kommende Arbeitskräfte an, hier ließen sich Gauner und arme Schlucker nieder, die In Odessa etwas Besseres erhofften. Insbesondere in den Jahren um 1900 und danach war der Anteil der jüdischen Bevölkerung sehr hoch. In diesem Stadtteil sucht man vergebens die Prachtbauten, wie sie im Zentrum zu sehen sind. Manch ein Industriegebäude erlebte hier zwar seine Blüte, doch ist davon kaum etwas übriggeblieben.

Nowadays the '7th km', which is situated next to the seven-kilometre-marker of a major main road, is the most important wholesale market in the Ukraine. A town within a town, a market with its own road system, it is full of shops and even has a small medical centre of its own. The stocks are kept in metal shipping containers which are piled on top of one another. Quite frequently, rock bands from Russia perform open-air-concerts here on summer evenings. Every day, around five hundred lorries and busses bring merchants from all over the Ukraine here to stock up on goods bought cheaply and in bulk by the wholesalers. A particularly great section features goods from Turkey which are somehow smuggled past the customs authorities. The '7th km' provides work to several thousand people from Odessa and the surrounding areas. This is of considerable economic importance, considering the high unemployment rate and the low level of income. The market provides the city with huge financial benefits and, as many insiders know, is also a source of extra income for quite a few civil servants. "They all have a finger in the pie: Customs, militia, nobody knows for certain who earns what here and by which means."

The route back into town leads through the Moldavanka, the famous quarter where the writer Isaac Babel lived. From the beginning of the nineteenth century onwards, workers from Moldova settled in the Moldavanka area, then small-time criminals and poor folk hoping to start a new life in Odessa moved in here. Particularly around the turn of the nineteenth and in the early years of the twentieth century, the Jewish contingent in the population was substantial. The magnificent buildings common in the town centre are absent from this part of town. Although quite a few industrial enterprises thrived here, hardly anything is left of this era.

Mode und Lifestyle liegen im Trend.
Fashion and life-styles are all the rage.

Die ‚Shustow‘-Fabrik:
Über 100 Jahre Kognak-Erfahrung
The ‘Shustov’ factory: more than
100 years of experience producing brandy

Prüfender Blick:
Kognak-Experte Arkadi Feuerstein
Taking a close look:
the brandy expert Arkady Feuerstein

Aber es gibt Ausnahmen. Eine heißt ‚Shustow'. Dahinter verbirgt sich der Name einer bedeutenden Kognakfabrik mit über 100-jähriger Tradition. Das helle Gebäude an der Hauptstraße fällt in dem Grau der niedrigen Häuser auf. ‚Shustow'-Kognak aus Odessa zählte zusammen mit den kaukasischen Konkurrenten aus Tiflis und Jerewan schon zur Zarenzeit zu den drei Besten. Stolz ist man auf internationale Preise, die auf Messen in Frankreich oder Spanien verliehen wurden. Heute liegt der Erfolg in den langjährigen Erfahrungen, den besten einheimischen Rohstoffen und modernster westlicher Technologie. Aus den Kognakfässern des Staatsbetriebes ‚Shustow' stammen rund 70 Prozent des offiziell in der Ukraine hergestellten, edlen Getränks. Die Alkoholproduktion lag seit je her in den Händen des Staates. Und deshalb sieht man mit wachsender Besorgnis die Zunahme der Schwarzbrennerei und die Herstellung von Plagiaten in großem Maßstab. Zum einen entstehen riesige ökonomische Verluste, zum anderen ist schon manch Trunkenbold an billigem Fusel erblindet oder gar gestorben.

Natürlich kann sich ein normaler Bürger keinen 15-jährigen Kognak für umgerechnet 50 Euro leisten. Doch was ist schon ein normaler Bürger? Man trifft immer mehr der sogenannten ‚Neuen Reichen' in der Stadt. Man erkennt sie an ihrer Kleidung, ihrem Auftreten und ihrem Auto, wobei Audi, BMW, Mercedes und Porsche auch in Odessa Lieblingsmarken zu sein scheinen. Ihr Geld stammt nicht unbedingt aus diversen Ölgeschäften, dem lukrativen Verkauf ehemaligen sowjetischen Eigentums an ausländische Firmen oder aus korrupten Machenschaften der kommunistischen Ära. Immer mehr Menschen sahen nach der Perestroika für sich die Chance, etwas Eigenes aufzubauen. Kleine Betriebe wurden größer und erste Profite zur Erweiterung der Firma eingesetzt.

There are exceptions: one is called 'Shustov'. This name stands for a well known type of brandy with a hundred-year tradition. The brightly painted building stands out between the low grey houses along the main street. 'Shustov' brandy from Odessa was considered one of the three best in the country even in the tsars' day, vying for top place with its Caucasian rivals from Tiflis and Erevan. The firm is particularly proud of prizes won at international shows in France and Spain. The brand's continuing success is due to a combination of years of experience, the best ingredients available locally and modern western technology. Seventy percent of the Ukraine's official production of the fortified wine comes from the casks of the state owned 'Shustov' factory. The production of alcoholic drinks has always been the prerogative of the state. The rise in illegal distilling and the large scale production of pirated products is therefore viewed with mounting disquiet. For one thing, these lead to huge economic losses, for the other, the risk of going blind or even dying is not inconsiderable with some of the cheap homebrews consumed by unfortunate Ukrainian alcoholics.

Of course a normal citizen can't afford a fifteen-year-old brandy at a price of around fifty euros. But what is a normal citizen? The number of 'nouveaux riches' that can be seen around town is on the increase. They are easily recognised by their clothes, their self-confidence and

Alexander Lipovoy: Mittelständischer Unternehmer im Aufbruch

Alexander Lipovoy: an entrepreneur on the way up

Alexander Lipovoy hat eine Schneiderei für Berufsbekleidung mit ungefähr 80 Angestellten. Er ist ein typischer Vertreter für einen aufstrebenden Mittelstand, von dem es in der Ukraine noch viel zu wenig gibt. Sein Erfolgsrezept: Für die Produktion von spezieller Berufsbekleidung verwendet er ausschließlich hochqualitative Materialien und Maschinen, wobei die meisten aus Westeuropa kommen. Aus Odessa will er aber niemals weg: „Ich bin Odessit, mein Vater war einer und mein Großvater auch. Es ist lustig hier und die Stadt fängt an aufzublühen, sie wird immer schöner, die Leute haben ihren Spaß und sind lustig. Ich hoffe, Odessa wird einmal so, wie ich es mir wünsche."

their cars, Audi, BMW, Mercedes and Porsche being the favourite brands in Odessa. Their money does not necessarily come from various oil deals, the financially rewarding sale of formally Soviet property to foreign firms or corrupt and shady dealings during the communist era. A growing number of people took the chance to start up a business of their own after the end of communism. Small firms grew and profits were reinvested to extend business operations.

Alexander Lipovoy runs a clothes factory with about eighty workers specialising in work clothing. He is a typical member of the group of entrepreneurs running medium sized firms whose confidence is growing, but of whom there are still far too few. His recipe for success: For the production of clothing specially designed for the needs of various types of jobs he uses only high quality material and machines, most of which come from the West. He firmly intends to stay in Odessa, however, "I am an Odessite, my father and grandfather were, too. It is fun to live here and the city is beginning to blossom, it is getting nicer by the day, people have fun, the mood is excellent. I hope Odessa will grow into the city I would wish for."

122

**Seit über zehn Jahren: Regensburger Hilfe
für Kinder und Kranke der Partnerstadt**
*More than ten years of aid and support for the children
and sick from the twin town of Regensburg*

**Obdachlosigkeit, Armut und Hunger:
Insbesondere ältere Bürger sind betroffen.**
*Homelessness, destitution and hunger:
The older citizens are particularly affected.*

Viele Menschen finden es in Odessa allerdings gar nicht lustig. Trotz Glanz und Glitter mancherorts begegnet man auf Schritt und Tritt Elend und Armut. Da sind bettelnde Kinder im Restaurant oder die vielen, meist älteren Menschen, die in Mülltonnen nach brauchbaren Dingen stochern. Es gibt in Odessa derart arme Gegenden, abseits der touristischen Attraktionen, wo sogar die Mülltonnen leer sind.

Und es gibt unzählige Obdachlose, Waisenkinder, Aids- und Tuberkulosekranke, denen nur wenig geholfen werden kann. Die Mittel der Stadt reichen nicht aus, auch nicht die der internationalen Hilfsorganisationen oder kirchlichen Verbände.

Zusätzliche Hilfe kommt seit über zehn Jahren aus der deutschen Partnerstadt Regensburg. Zum einen fahren regelmäßig Hilfstransporte mit Lebensmitteln, Bekleidung oder Kleinmöbeln für Krankenhäuser und Kinderheime nach Odessa, zum anderen wird aus Regensburg die Rehabilitationsstation ‚Goldener Engel' mit medizinischen und physiotherapeutischen Geräten unterstützt. Initiator des ‚Goldenen Engel' ist der ehemals erfolgreiche Boxer und jetzige Leiter einer Sportschule in Odessa, Boris Litvak. Seine Tochter starb an einem Krebsleiden. Vor ihrem Tod bat sie ihren Vater, dass er sich in Zukunft nicht nur um die Gesunden und sportlich Besten kümmere, sondern auch um kranke und behinderte Kinder. Ohne die Unterstützung aus Regensburg, davon ist Boris Litvak überzeugt, hätte er den Wunsch seiner Tochter nicht realisieren können.

Lebensrettende Hilfe kommt in dringenden Fällen auf vier Rädern. Seit dem Jahre 1903 gibt es in Odessa die ‚Schnelle Medizinische Hilfe' (SMH) – damals mit natürlichen Pferdestärken. Heute rasen die Fahrzeuge der SMH Odessa motorgetrieben über die Schlaglöcher der Straßen, darunter auch modern ausgestattete Rettungswagen aus der Partnerstadt Regensburg.

Many people however do not find Odessa great fun. In spite of the bright, shiny new developments, poverty and destitution are everpresent around town. The children begging in the restaurants and the elderly people grubbing around the rubbish bins for something usable come to mind. There are districts of Odessa, far away from the tourist venues, which are so poor that even the dustbins are empty.

There is an uncounted number of homeless, orphans, people suffering from AIDS or tuberculosis who receive insufficient support. The city's funds don't cover the cost and neither do the funds of international aid agencies or church organisations.

Added help has been brought to the city for the last ten years from the German twin-town of Regensburg. For one thing, there are regular convoys to Odessa, carrying food, clothing and small items of furniture for the hospitals and orphanages, for the other the 'Golden Angel', a day clinic for the rehabilitation of sick children, is supplied with medical aid and instruments for physiotherapy treatments. The initiative for the 'Golden Angel' came from Boris Litvak, once a successful boxer, now head of a sports school in Odessa. His daughter died of cancer. Before her death she asked her father to give his support not just to the fittest and most able, but to look after sick and disabled children as well. Boris Litvak is certain that without the help from Regensburg he would not have been able to put into practice his daughter's dying wish.

In urgent cases, life saving aid comes on four wheels. Odessa has had an ambulance service since 1903, although in those days the ambulances were of course driven by real horse power. Nowadays the ambulances race around the city, regardless of the many potholes, under their own steam. Some of them are well equipped modern vehicles donated by the twin-town Regensburg.

Ob mit Luxuswagen oder der Tram durch die Stadt: Trittbrettfahrer haben den meisten Spaß.
Whether travelling by luxury limousine or by tram: Joy-riders have most fun.

Troika:

Wenn sich drei zusammenfinden

Troika:

Two is company, three is a joint venture

Ein Drei-Männer-Gremium zwischen Politikern wird im Russischen als Troika bezeichnet – wie z.B. das Bündnis zwischen Stalin, Kamenjew und Sinowjew gegen Trotzki. Im ursprünglichen Sinn ist eine Troika ein Gespann aus drei Pferden, die einen Schlitten oder eine Kutsche ziehen. Eine spezielle Variante der Troika sah man zu Sowjetzeiten häufig vor Schnapsläden, in Parkanlagen und in Hinterhöfen. Drei Rubel für eine Flasche Wodka war meist zuviel für eine Person. Daher suchte ein ‚Durstiger‘ durch Hochhalten zweier Finger ‚Gleichgesinnte‘, die dann jeder einen Rubel in den Hut warfen (umgangssprachlich: ‚po rublju‘). Danach konnte die Pulle kreisen. Mit dieser typisch russischen Geschichte im Hinterkopf stechen gerade Dreiergruppen dem aufmerksamen Beobachter sofort ins Auge, obwohl diese Art der ‚Wodkabeschaffungsmaßnahme‘ heute nur noch selten im Straßenbild von Odessa zu sehen ist.

A three-man-alliance between politicians is known as a troika in Russian – a famous example being the alliance between Stalin, Kamenev and Sinovev to oust Trotsky. In its original meaning, a troika is a group of three horses pulling a sleigh or carriage. A different kind of troika was to be observed frequently during the Soviet era outside the shops selling vodka, in parks or backyards of houses. Three roubles for a bottle of vodka tended to be to expensive for an individual buyer. Therefore 'thirsty' Russians would try to find 'business partners' by holding up two fingers, each of the partners would then contribute one rouble (the slang expression being 'po rublju'). The bottle purchased would be passed round. With this typical situation in mind, an observant visitor will of course notice a wide variety of groups of three around the city, although the 'vodka joint ventures' have nearly disappeared from the streets.

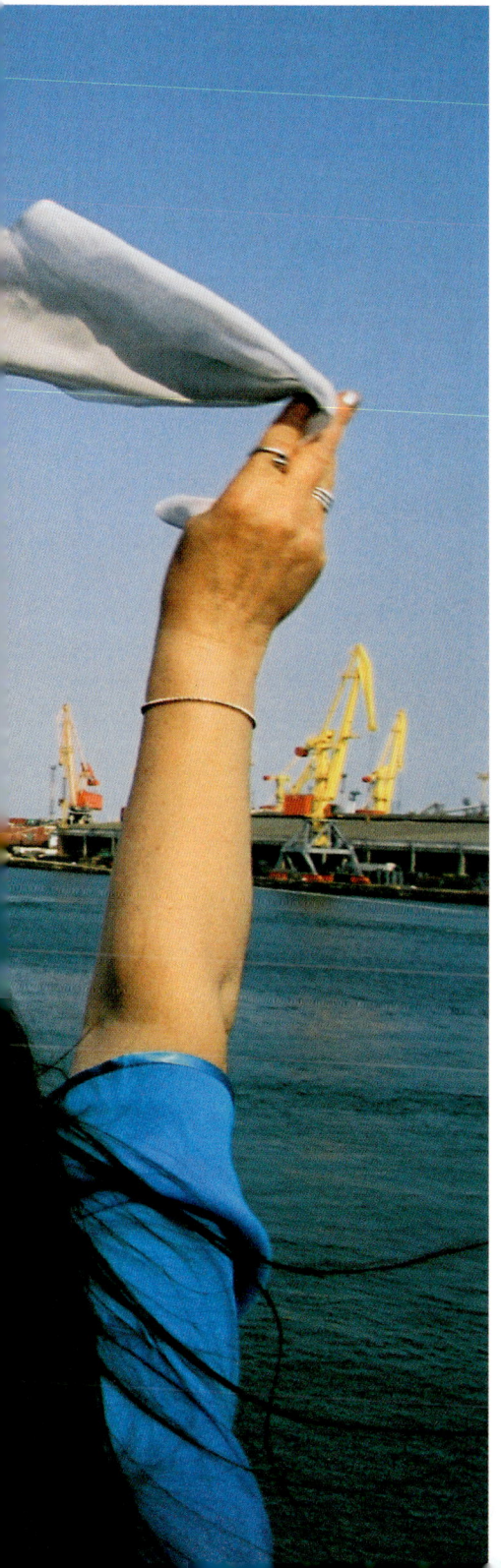

WWW:

„Odessiten aller Länder vereinigt Euch!"

WWW:

"Odessites of the world unite!"

Eine der prägnanten Eigenschaften des ‚Homo odessiensis' ist sein Witz und Humor, der mit einer skurrilen Gelassenheit – für manche Mitteleuropäer unerträgliche – Situationen meistert. Eine kleine Kostprobe: Es ist heiß, ein Großraumtaxi mit acht Sitzplätzen in der Nähe des ‚Privoz' – Rush Hour! Ständig zwängen sich zu- und aussteigende Personen unterschiedlicher Körperfülle aneinander vorbei, durchschnittlich zwölf Fahrgäste befinden sich im Wagen. Der Fahrer macht seine Witzchen und warnt jeden Neuankömmling: Wegen einer Straßensperrung mache er einen Umweg und es sei ein Experiment, sein Taxi zu nehmen. Alle 100 Meter muss er anhalten, um Kühlwasser aufzufüllen. Eine klapprige Straßenbahn im Rückspiegel drängelt bimmelnd. Zwei junge Frauen auf den hinteren Sitzen gackern wie die Hühner, eine Alte schubst, die Luft wird immer dicker, draußen herrschen 30°C – alle bleiben gelassen. Nur ein etwas älterer Herr rutscht unruhig auf seinem Platz hin und her und verlässt bei der nächsten Gelegenheit das Großraumtaxi. Der trockene Kommentar des Fahrers: „Wieder einer, der das Experiment nicht ausgehalten hat!". Schallendes Gelächter.

One of the most striking features of 'homo odessiensis' is a sense of humour, paired with a weirdly laid-back attitude to situations which most Western Europeans would find unbearable. A quick sample. It is hot and sticky on the eight-seater minibus service running past 'Privoz', the middle of rush hour! Constantly, passengers of varying sizes and circumferences push past each other, trying to get in and out. There is an average of twelve passengers on the bus at any one time. The driver makes little jokes and warns every new arrival that due to a closed road he is going to have to make a detour and that travelling with him means taking part in an experiment. Every hundred metres he has to stop to fill up the water in the radiator. An ancient tram wobbles up to the back bumper and impatiently rings its bell. Two young girls on the back seat giggle away like a pair of hens, an old woman constantly shoves everyone, the airlessness on the bus increases, outside, the temperature is above 30°C – but everyone stays calm. Only one elderly gentleman fidgets in his seat and gets off the bus at the earliest possible stop. Upon which the driver dryly comments, "That one has failed the experiment!" The comment is greeted with great hilarity.

Situations such as these are common in everyday life which is not by any means always an easy ride. Nevertheless, a special brand of humour has developed in the city, perhaps because people of varying nationalities have always lived together peacefully and each nation has contributed its jokes to the big melting-pot of Odessa humour. The many artists who moved to Odessa may also have contributed: Ilv, Petrov, Babel or, to mention a present day author, Zhvanetsky.

The high point of the year is April 1st, when the whole city gears up for 'Humorina-day', a festival dedicated to jokes and fun. There are street parades, fancy dress, satire and comedy shows, beach parties, special exhibitions on caricature, concerts, basically: The whole town has a huge party which goes on until late at

Ähnliche Situationen sind keine Seltenheit im täglichen Leben, das wahrlich nicht immer leicht ist. Dennoch hat sich in der Stadt ein eigener Humor herausgebildet, vielleicht weil schon immer Menschen der unterschiedlichsten Nationalitäten friedlich miteinander lebten und jede Nation ihren Witz in den großen Schmelztiegel Odessa geworfen hat. Vielleicht haben auch die zahlreichen Künstler, die es hierher zog, einen Teil dazu beigetragen: Ilf, Petrow, Babel oder der Zeitgenosse Schwanetzki.

Höhepunkt der guten Laune ist alljährlich der 1. April, dann feiert die ganze Stadt die ,Humorina', den Tag des Ulks und des Frohsinns. Straßenumzüge, lustige Kostüme, Satireveranstaltungen, Strandfeste, Sonderausstellungen über Karikatur, spezielle Konzerte, kurz: Rambazamba überall und bis in die späte Nacht! Nunmehr seit 30 Jahren begeht Odessa sein Fest des Lachens und neuerdings wird jedes Jahr zur ,Humorina' ein kleines Denkmal für ein Odessaer Original im Park hinter dem Literaturmuseum eingeweiht. Hier stehen Figuren wie die ,Odessa-Mama', der ,Rabinovitsch', ,Sascha-Musikant' oder das ,Denkmal für ein zukünftiges Genie' auf ihrem Sockel.

night! The festival has been celebrated for thirty years now and the newest feature is the inauguration of a small monument to a popular Odessite personality, which takes place every year in the park behind the Museum of Literature. Memorials have been erected for figures such as 'Odessa-Mama', 'Rabinovitch', 'Sacha the Musician' and 'a future genius'.

Odessa-Mama:
Symbolfigur der Stadt
Odessa-Mama:
the symbol of the city

Vor dem Büro des ‚Weltclubs der Odessiten':
Jewgeni Golubowski
Jevgeni Golubovsky outside the office
of the 'World Club of Odessites'

Natalja Koslowa:
Chefredakteurin
der Zeitschrift ‚Passage'
Natalja Koslova:
editor of the
'Passage' magazine

Als Odessa vor über 200 Jahren gegründet wurde, war der Ort Anziehungspunkt für Menschen aus ganz Europa. Heute ist die Schwarzmeermetropole eine Stadt der Auswanderer. Es gibt keinen Kontinent auf der Welt, auf dem nicht Menschen leben, die den Duft der Akazien am Primorski Boulevard eingeatmet haben. War Odessa zur Zeit der Sowjetunion der Ort, von dem viele Juden nach Israel ausgewandert sind, so heißen die Ziele derjenigen, die eine neue Zukunft suchen, jetzt auch New York, Paris, Berlin oder Sydney. Die meisten von ihnen fühlen sich in ihrem Inneren aber noch als Odessiten, wie man in vielen Internetforen nachlesen kann. So entstand 1990 die Idee, den ‚Weltclub der Odessiten' zu gründen. Sein Vorsitzender ist der

When Odessa was founded 200 years ago, the place drew people from all over Europe. Today, the city on the Black Sea is a city of émigrés: there is no continent on the face of this earth that is not home to people who once breathed the perfume of the white acacias on Primorsky Boulevard. In Soviet times, many Jews left Odessa to start a new life in Israel; nowadays many of those leaving the city for a brighter future are heading for New York, Berlin or Sydney. Most of them, however, continue to consider themselves Odessites, a fact that is emphasised by the numerous topical internet sites. Because Odessites tend to be so attached to their old home the idea was born in 1990 for the 'World Club of Odessites'. The president of the club is the popular writer and satirist Michail Zhvanetsky. He is so popular he already has had a 'Humorina-monument' dedicated to him.

The central bureau of the 'World Club of Odessites' is an office close to 'Privoz' market, but there are also branch offices in the US, Germany and Moscow. Information is circulated by way of the 'Worldwide Odessa News', run by the journalist Jevgeni Golubovsky. Both the club and the paper have a very modest goal, printed in small letters across the top of every edition: "Odessites of the world unite!"

populäre Schriftsteller und Satiriker Michail Schwanetzki. Er ist derart beliebt, dass er bereits als ‚Humorina-Denkmal' hinter dem Literaturmuseum steht.

Die Zentrale des ‚Weltclubs der Odessiten' ist ein Büro in der Nähe vom ‚Privoz', es gibt aber auch Außenstellen in den USA, Deutschland und in Moskau. Sprachrohr ist die monatlich erscheinende Clubzeitung ‚Weltweite Odessaer Nachrichten', die von dem Journalisten Jewgeni Golubowski geleitet wird. Sowohl der Club wie auch seine Zeitung haben ein bescheidenes Ziel, das in kleinen Buchstaben auf jeder Titelseite steht: „Odessiten aller Länder vereinigt Euch!"

Erst seit kurzem ist der ‚Weltclub' auch im Internet mit einer Homepage präsent. Auf www.odessitclub.org wird der Surfer mit den Worten begrüßt:
„… Juden, Russen, Ukrainer, Griechen Moldawier!
Was habt Ihr noch außer Odessa in Eurer Seele?
Sie – die Mama! …
Und damit ist unsere Webseite für alle offen.
Wir werden die Hälfte des Erdballs in Atem halten,
diese Hälfte nennt sich … Odessa."

Auf den Internetseiten findet man zahlreiche Artikel zur Stadtgeschichte, über Kunst, Architektur und zum Zeitgeist. Dazu kommen Clubnachrichten und Aktuelles aus dem Stadtleben, Kostproben des Satirikers Schwanetzki im Originalton sowie viele Lieder über Odessa. Die Internetseite ist in Russisch und in Englisch, mit ausreichender Sprachkenntnis findet man garantiert interessante Infos.

www.odessaglobe.com ist eine der informativsten und vielseitigsten Internetadressen für die Stadt. In Russisch und Englisch bietet die Seite aktuelle Informationen zum Stadtgeschehen – von der großen Politik bis zur kleineren Kunstausstellung. Enthalten sind auch praktische Hinweise für eine eventuelle Reiseplanung: Das aktuelle Wetter, ein Stadtplan, Geschichten zu Persönlichkeiten der Stadt, ein Karten- und Hotelservice. Die historische Altstadt ist virtuell begehbar und die Seite hält einen Museumsführer bereit, ebenso wie eine Sammlung Odessaer Witze.

Die Idee zu diesem Internetangebot kam von Juri Sychev und Anatoly Kontusch, ehemaligen Physik-Studenten der ‚Metschnikov'-Universität. Beide waren Teilnehmer an den Satire-Wettbewerben, die alljährlich

Only recently, the 'World Club' has acquired a web site. Web-surfers are welcomed to the homepage at www.odessitclub.org with the following words,
"… Jews, Russians, Ukrainians, Greeks, Moldovans!
What does your soul yearn for apart from Odessa?
Right – Mama! …
And hereby we declare our website open to all.
We will make sure half of the world is waiting with bated breath,
The half called … Odessa!"

The website contains many articles on city history, art, architecture and the zeitgeist. Additionally, there is club news and gossip about the life of the city. There are also samples of Zhvanetzky reading his own work and lots of songs about Odessa to listen to. The site is in Russian and English. Those with a reasonable grasp of the languages, however, are sure to find interesting information.

www.odessaglobe.com is one of the internet sites that offers the widest range of information on the city. The site is kept up-to-date with news on the life of the city – from big politics to small exhibitions. There is also a supply of information useful for planning a possible trip to Odessa: weather news, a map of the city, stories on city personalities and a booking service for tickets and accommodation. You can take a virtual stroll around the old city centre and there is a guide to the museums as well as a collection of Odessite jokes. The internet service is based on an idea by Yury Sychev and Anatoly Kontush, formerly students of physics at the city's 'Mechnikov'-University. Both were regular participants in the annual satire competitions between the staff and the students. Yury now lives in New York and is a comedian, Anatoly works as a scientist in Hamburg and Paris.

zwischen Studenten und Dozenten veranstaltet werden. Juri lebt heute als Kabarettist in New York, Anatoly arbeitet als Wissenschaftler in Hamburg und Paris.

Die meisten anderen Internetseiten sind bescheidener in ihren Angeboten, allerdings kann man durchaus spezielle Leckerbissen finden. Einen solchen bietet www.odessit.com. Gemeint sind nicht unbedingt die Küchenrezepte, sondern ein umfangreiches Synonymwörterbuch der besonderen Art. Es vergleicht in mehreren hundert Beispielen russische Wörter und Redewendungen mit dem typisch Odessaer Pendant. Fragt man z.B. auf russisch: *„Wie kommt man am besten zur Deribassowskaja?"*, so würde ein Odessit fragen: *„Wo hinein muss ich mich setzen, um zur Deribassowskaja zu gelangen?"*

Der Leuchtturm des Hafens von Odessa ist auch ein Wegweiser auf www.odessaweb.info. Er führt den Besucher durch eine Fotogalerie und zu Liedern über die Stadt.

Redlich müht sich das Stadtjournal ‚Passage', Menschen aus aller Welt in die Stadt zu locken. *„Wir wollen der Halbinsel Krim als Tourismuszentrum Paroli bieten"*, sagt die Chefredakteurin Natalja Koslowa. Das versucht die Monatszeitschrift mit jungen Models auf der Titelseite, mit Berichten über die Stadt, aber auch über gleichnamige Orte außerhalb der Ukraine, wie z.B. Odessa in den US-Bundesstaaten Washington und Texas oder das kleine Dorf Odessa in Brasilien. So umfangreich, aber mit Werbung überladen, wie die Zeitschrift ist auch das hauseigene Internetangebot www.odessapassage.com.

Most of the other websites are more modest in what they provide, but there are a few special tit-bits to be found. One of them is located on the website of www.odessit.com. And the reference is not to tit-bits in the culinary sense. The special feature of the site is a thesaurus, comparing several hundred Russian words and phrases with their Odessite counterparts. For example, whereas a Russian would ask, "What is the best way to get to Deribasovskaya?" an Odessite would enquire, "On what do I have to find a seat to get to Deribasovskaya?"

The lighthouse in Odessa harbour is used to guide visitors at www.odessaweb.info. It leads users through a gallery of photos and to songs about Odessa.

The city magazine 'Passage' valiantly tries to entice people from all over the world to Odessa. "We would like to compete for tourists with the Crimean peninsula", says editor Natalja Koslova. The magazine tries to achieve this by featuring pictures of youthful models on the cover, reports on the city and articles on places called Odessa outside Ukraine, for example the Odessas in the US states of Texas and Washington or the little village of Odessa in Brazil. The magazine's website, www.odessapassage.com, has just as much content as the magazine, but is overloaded with advertising.

Der Leuchtturm des Hafens: Wegweiser für Schiffe und Internetsurfer
The light house in the harbour: a guiding light for ships and web-surfers alike

**Ob mit Flugzeug oder Zug –
herzlich willkommen in Odessa.**
*Whether you arrive by plane or train –
a warm welcome to Odessa.*

Wichtige Tipps: Von A bis Z

Important information: an Odessa A to Z

Arriving in Odessa

Western Europeans need to purchase a visa. This costs around fifty euros and is issued by the Ukrainian embassies and consulates. Since 2002 it has also become possible to obtain a visa at Odessa airport.

Several international airlines fly to Odessa on a regular basis: 'Austrian Airlines' fly from Vienna, 'Malev' from Budapest, 'LOT' from Warsaw and various Turkish airlines from Istanbul. There are also flight connections from capitals such as Moscow, Kiev and Chisinau (Moldova). A return flight from Germany costs around four hundred euros. The train journey from Kiev to Odessa takes around nine hours. There are direct coach lines run by various firms from major German cities to Odessa (from around one hundred and fifty euros, taking about thirty hours). For security reasons we would not recommend travelling by private car. A particularly attractive route is to fly to Istanbul and then travel by ship to Odessa.

Anreise

Für Westeuropäer besteht Visapflicht. Ein Touristenvisum kostet ca. 50 Euro und wird in der ukrainischen Botschaft oder in Konsulaten ausgestellt. Seit 2002 kann man das Einreisevisum auch auf dem Odessaer Flughafen erhalten.

Derzeit fliegen mehrere internationale Fluggesellschaften Odessa an: Die ‚Austrian Airlines' von Wien, ‚Malev' von Budapest, ‚LOT' von Warschau und türkische Gesellschaften von Istanbul. Dazu kommen Flugverbindungen aus Hauptstädten wie Moskau, Kiew, Chisinau (Moldawien). Hin- und Rückflug von Deutschland aus gibt es ab 400 Euro. Mit dem Zug kommt man von Kiew nach Odessa in ca. neun Stunden. Verschiedene Busunternehmen bieten aus größeren Städten in Deutschland Direktverbindungen an (ab 150 Euro, Fahrtdauer ca. 30 Stunden). Privatreisen mit dem Auto werden aus Sicherheitsgründen nicht empfohlen. Ein Reisetipp der besonderen Art: Bis Istanbul per Flugzeug und dann mit dem Schiff nach Odessa.

Allgemeines

Odessa liegt an der Nordwestküste des Schwarzen Meeres und ist der mitteleuropäischen Zeit um eine Stunde voraus. Das Stromnetz hat 220 Volt, Flachstecker am Rasierapparat oder Fön passen. Brief- bzw. Postsendungen dauern ungefähr eine Woche bis zum Empfänger im Ausland. Telefonieren, bevorzugt mit Karte, ist kein Problem, das Funknetz für Mobiltelefon (GSM) ist stabil. Die akustische Qualität lässt jedoch zu wünschen übrig. Der Ländercode für die Ukraine ist 0038, für Odessa ist 0482 zu wählen.

Ausflüge

Lohnenswerte Kurzreisen bieten Reiseunternehmen vor Ort u.a. zur Halbinsel Krim, ins Donaudelta und zur Festungsruine ‚Tyros' nach Belgorod-Dnestrowski.

Banken & Geld

Die Landeswährung heißt Griwna, der Wechselkurs zum Dollar beträgt ungefähr 5:1. Devisentausch ist in allen Banken, aber auch in kleineren Wechselstellen ohne Probleme möglich, genauso auch der Geldwechsel an Bankautomaten. Kreditkarten wie American Express, Visa-, Euro- oder Master-Card werden akzeptiert.

Einkaufen

Das Angebot in Geschäften und Supermärkten umfasst einheimische Produkte sowie Importwaren aus Westeuropa. Supermärkte haben bis in die späten Abendstunden geöffnet, kleinere Geschäfte sogar rund um die Uhr. Für Touristen ist der Markt ‚Privoz' ein ‚Muss'. Er befindet sich in der Nähe des Hauptbahnhofes. Der Großhandelsmarkt ‚Siebter Kilometer', etwas außerhalb der Stadt ist eine ‚Shopping-Attraktion' für Neugierige. Souvenirs kauft man am besten auf der Deribassowskaja und dem Kunstmarkt.

Banking & Money

The Ukrainian currency is called grivna, the exchange rate with the dollar is approximately 5:1. All banks and also smaller exchange bureaus will exchange foreign currency with no trouble whatsoever, cash machines are also readily available. American Express, Visa, Euro and Mastercards are all accepted.

Catacombs

By quarrying sedimentary limestone for building material, an underground maze of nearly two thousand kilometres in length was created. The catacombs were used as a hide-out by the partisans in World War II. Tourist visits are now possible from two locations: the Museum of Art and a memorial outside the city.

Climate & Weather

The region's climate is dry, continental and not too extreme. The winters are short and comparatively mild. The average temperature in January is –2°C. The summer is pleasantly warm, sometimes quite hot, with temperatures averaging around 24°C. Top temperatures up to 40°C are possible.

Customs

When entering the country, it is a good idea to declare valuables and cash worth more than one thousand euros on your customs declaration form. Importing literature or newspapers with anti-Ukrainian content is illegal. If you buy valuable items, keep the bill, you may be asked to present it on departure. There may be weight limits for air travel. Make sure you keep to the restrictions, as excess baggage tends to be expensive. It may be a good idea to buy heavy vodka bottles in the duty-free-area after checking in your luggage!

Excursions

Local travel agencies offer worthwhile excursions, e.g. to the Crimean peninsula, to the Danube estuary or to the ruin of the 'Tyros' fortress in Belgorod-Dnestrovski.

Essen & Trinken

In den letzten Jahren sind in Odessa viele Restaurants entstanden. Als weltoffene Stadt bietet man sowohl ukrainische wie internationale Küche an. In besseren Gaststätten wird die Speisekarte auch in englischer Sprache gereicht. Die Gerichte und der Service sind gut, das Preis-Leistungs-Verhältnis ist sehr attraktiv. Das ‚Lakomka' auf der Deribassowskaja und das ‚Chutorok' in der Nähe des ‚Langeron'-Strandes sind empfehlenswerte Restaurants mit ukrainischen Spezialitäten. Das Trinkgeld von fünf bis zehn Prozent lässt man nach Erhalt des Wechselgeldes liegen.

Hotels

Traditionsreiche Hotels sind das ‚Londonskaja' und das ‚Krasnaja', beide Vier-Sterne-Hotels. Als einziges Hotel hat das ‚Odessa' einen Stern mehr, einen Hauch von ‚K- und K-Atmosphäre' verbreitet das neu erbaute ‚Mozart' gegenüber dem Operntheater. Aktuelle Informationen zu den jeweiligen Angeboten und Preisen erhält man auf verschiedenen Internetseiten.

Internet

Die besten Informationen (englisch) im ‚world wide web' findet man auf odessaglobe.com und odessitclub.org. Aktuelle Veranstaltungshinweise und Lokales bietet u.a. passage.com.

Katakomben

Durch den Abbau von Muschelkalkstein als Baumaterial entstand ein unterirdisches Labyrinth von fast 2000 Kilometern. Die Katakomben dienten im Zweiten Weltkrieg den Partisanen als Versteck. Zu besichtigen sind sie heute an zwei Stellen: Im Kunstmuseum und in einer Gedenkstätte außerhalb der Stadt.

Klima & Wetter

Das Gebiet besitzt ein gemäßigtes, trockenes Kontinentalklima. Der Winter ist kurz und relativ mild. Die mittlere Temperatur im Januar beträgt –2°C. Der Sommer ist angenehm warm bis heiß mit Durchschnittstemperaturen um 24°C. Spitzenwerte bis 40°C sind möglich.

Medizinische Versorgung

Sollte nur in Ausnahmefällen in Anspruch genommen werden. Die Ausstattung der Krankenhäuser ist meist dürftig, die Medikamentenversorgung der zahlreichen Apotheken dagegen gut. Fast alle Arzneimittel sind frei verkäuflich. Odessa hat die höchste Aids-Rate in der Ukraine.

Museum

Das kulturelle Angebot in den zahlreichen Museen der Stadt ist sehr umfangreich, die Eintrittspreise sind niedrig. Von überregionaler Bedeutung sind das Literaturmuseum, das Kunstmuseum, das Archäologische Museum, das ‚Puschkin'-Museum, das Schifffahrtsmuseum und das Museum für Orientalische und Westeuropäische Kunst. Empfehlenswert ist auch ein Besuch im Wachsfigurenkabinett. Fast alle wichtigen Museen befinden sich im Stadtzentrum.

Musik und Theater

Weltklasse für wenige Euro bieten die Bühnen der Stadt. Allen voran das architektonisch berühmte Operntheater mit einem breiten Repertoire klassischer Meister.
Die Konzerte der Odessaer Philharmonie sind über die Stadtgrenzen hinweg bekannt und beliebt. Modernes Theater wird u.a. in der Musikalischen Komödie gegeben. Will man Szene-Musik (Jazz und Folk) erleben, muss man vor Ort fragen.

Food & Drink

Over the last few years, many new restaurants have opened up in Odessa. Being a cosmopolitan city, Odessa has both Ukrainian and international cuisine on offer. Better quality eating places are able to provide a menu in English. The food and service are good, the prices very reasonable indeed. Good places for sampling Ukrainian cookery are the 'Lakomka' on Deribasovskaya and the 'Khutorok' close to 'Langeron' beach. A tip, usually around five to ten percent of the bill, is left on the table after the staff has brought the change.

General Information

Odessa is situated on the north western coast of the Black Sea and is two hours ahead of GMT, one hour ahead of central European time. The electricity system runs at 220 Volt, Central European type flat electrical plugs on shavers or hairdryers will fit. Mail sent by post takes around a week to reach a foreign address. Telephones, especially card phones, are readily available, the cell phone net (GSM-net) is stable, though the quality of transmission is not very satisfactory. The dialling code for Ukraine is 0038, the Odessa code is 0482.

Hotels

The 'Londonskaya' and the 'Krasnaya', both of them four-star establishments, are hotels with long traditions to look back on. The only five-star hotel is the 'Odessa'. The newly erected 'Mozart' opposite the opera house has a touch of Austro-Hungarian Empire to it. Various web sites offer up-to-date information on availability and rates.

Internet

The best information (in English) is available at odessaglobe.com and odessitclub.org. Up-to-the-minute information on events and items of local interest are provided by passage.com, for example.

Medical facilities

Should only be used in an emergency. The hospitals are usually very poorly equipped. The many pharmacies on the other hand offer a full range of medication. Practically all types of medication are available without a prescription. Odessa has the highest HIV-rate in the Ukraine.

Museums

The variety of exhibitions on offer at the city's many museums is substantial, the entrance fees very low. The Museum of Literature, the Museum of Art, the Archaeological Museum, the 'Pushkin' Museum, the Museum of Shipping and the Museum of Oriental and Western European Art are of more than just regional importance. A visit to the waxworks is also worthwhile. Nearly all the better known museums are in the centre of town.

Music & Theatre

The city's venues offer world class performances at very low prices. The foremost venue is of course the opera house which offers magnificent architecture along with a wide repertoire of classical masterpieces. Concerts given by the Odessa Philharmonic are well known and popular beyond the city limits. More modern shows are presented at the Musical Comedy Theatre, for example. For live acts, such as jazz or folk concerts, it is best to enquire on arrival.

Nachtleben

Die Nacht gehört vorwiegend der jüngeren Generation. Diskotheken, Varieté, Tanz und Unterhaltung finden in speziellen Clubs statt. Das Showtheater ‚Amsterdam' zählt mit dem ‚E', dem ‚Mirage' und dem Nachtclub ‚Rio' zu den ersten Adressen (Eintrittspreise um die zehn Euro). Tanz und Unterhaltung findet man aber auch in den Bars und Spielsalons der Hotels. Spezieller Tipp: Die Diskothek ‚Sportiwna' in der Nähe des Polytechnischen Instituts mit moderaten Preisen und jugendlicher Musik.

Strand und Meer

Badesaison ist von Mai bis September. Die wärmsten Monate sind der Juli und August mit einer durchschnittlichen Wassertemperatur von 23°C. Es gibt vorwiegend breite Sandstrände, die Uferzonen sind meist flach und der Wellengang ist aufgrund der geschützten Buchtlage nur gering. Der beliebteste Strand ist Arkadia.

Verkehrsmittel

Es besteht ein umfangreiches Straßenbahn- und Busnetz, das jedoch einer technischen Erneuerung bedarf. Der Fahrpreis beträgt 50 Kopeken, das sind weniger als zehn Cent. Ein offizielles Taxi erkennt man am entsprechenden Schild auf dem Autodach. Die Preise sind verhandelbar, man sollte aber vor Antritt der Fahrt wissen, wie viel für die Strecke verlangt wird. Die preiswerte Alternative dazu sind die zahlreichen ‚Schwarztaxen'. Hier bezahlt man nach eigenem Ermessen. Meist für eine oder zwei Griwna kann man ein Großraumtaxi nutzen. Die Fahrzeuge pendeln auf unterschiedlichen Routen. Sie werden daher auch ‚Marschrutni Taxi' genannt.

Nightlife

Mostly members of the younger generation are out and about in the night time. Club-nights, variety shows, dancing and entertainment takes place at specialised venues. The show-theatre 'Amsterdam', the 'E', the 'Mirage' and the 'Rio' night-clubs are among the best places to go. It will cost you around ten euros to get in. However, the bars and casinos of the hotels also offer dancing and entertainment. If you are travelling on a budget, the 'Sportivna' club situated near the Polytechnic Institute plays music aimed at a young audience and has kept its prices very reasonable.

Public Transport

There is a large net of tram and bus-lines which could however do with a thorough overhaul. The ticket price is fifty kopecks, less than ten euro cents. Official taxis carry a taxi-sign on their roofs. The prices can be negotiated, but it is advisable to know what the usual price for the route is before bargaining begins. The cheap option is the unofficial taxis, here prices are entirely up to the passengers. A trip on the minibus service costs about one or two grivna. The minibuses are known as 'Marshroutni taxis', as they run back and forth along certain routes, but have no fixed time-tables.

Zoll

Bei der Einreise ist es ratsam, mitgeführte Wertgegenstände und Bargeld über 1000 Euro bei der Zolldeklaration anzugeben. Es ist untersagt, Literatur oder Presseerzeugnisse mit antiukrainischen Inhalten einzuführen. Bei der Ausreise wird empfohlen, erworbene Wertgegenstände durch Kaufbelege nachweisen zu können. Bei Flugreisen ist auf eventuelle Gewichtsbeschränkungen für das Reisegepäck zu achten. Übergewicht kann sehr teuer werden. Tipp: Kaufen Sie die schwergewichtigen Wodkaflaschen nach der Zollabfertigung im Duty Free Shop!

Zickzack

Bevorzugte Fortbewegungsart auf der überfüllten Deribassowskaja und unbedingt zu empfehlen, wenn man sich in die Nebenstraßen begibt: Die zahlreichen Gullydeckel warten nur darauf, dass jemand auf sie tritt und auf Nimmerwiedersehen in die darunter gelegenen Katakomben fällt. Diese Story zählt jedoch zu den mehr oder weniger lustigen Stadtanekdoten und kommt bei Urlaubsgeschichten immer gut an.

Seaside & Beaches

The bathing season runs from May through to September. The warmest months are July and August, with an average water temperature of 23°C. Most of the beaches are wide and sandy, the water along the beaches relatively flat and the amount of surf very limited due to the situation within the bay. The most popular beach is Arcadia.

Shopping

The shops and supermarkets stock both local produce and imported goods from Western Europe. Supermarkets are open till late in the evening, smaller shops are frequently open twenty-four hours. A 'must-see' for tourists is the 'Privoz' market, which is close to the main railway station. The wholesale market 'Seventh Kilometre', situated a little way out of town, provides an unusual shopping experience for the adventurous. Souvenirs are best bought on Deribasovskaya or at the arts and crafts market.

Zigzag

The preferred mode of progress when dodging the crowds on Deribasovskaya and highly recommended in the side streets: The many man-hole covers are just waiting for someone to step on them and be swallowed up for ever by the catacombs underneath. This particular Odessite urban myth always works well when trying to make folks back home laugh!

Joachim Baumann, geboren 1954 in Weimar, studierte von 1973 bis 1978 Physik an der ‚Metschnikow'-Universität Odessa. Seit 1983 arbeitet er als Wissenschaftsredakteur für verschiedene Rundfunkanstalten, derzeit beim DeutschlandRadio Berlin.

Joachim Baumann, born in 1954 in Weimar, studied physics at Odessa's 'Metchnikov' University from 1973 to 1978. Since 1983 he has worked as a science correspondent for various radio stations. At present he is employed with DeutschlandRadio Berlin.

Uwe Moosburger, geboren 1964 in Neumarkt/Oberpfalz, absolvierte 1985/86 ein Volontariat bei der Mittelbayerischen Zeitung in Regensburg. Seit 1987 ist er dort als Redakteur und Bildjournalist tätig. 1999 Auszeichnung mit dem Eberhard-Woll-Preis des Regensburger Presseclubs.

Uwe Moosburger, born in 1964 in Neumarkt/Oberpfalz, trained as a journalist with the Mittelbayerische Zeitung in Regensburg from 1985 to 1986. Since 1987 he has worked for the newspaper as a journalist and press photographer. In 1999 he was winner of the Eberhard-Woll-Prize awarded by the Regensburg Press Club.